P9-EDM-958

The Gazer Within

The Gazer Within

Larry Levis

Edited by James Marshall,
Andrew Miller, and John Venable,
with the assistance of Mary Flinn

Ann Arbor

THE UNIVERSITY OF MICHIGAN PRESS

Copyright © by the University of Michigan 2001
All rights reserved
Published in the United States of America by
The University of Michigan Press
Manufactured in the United States of America
♾ Printed on acid-free paper

2004   2003   2002   2001   4   3   2   1

A CIP catalog record for this book is available from the British Library.

Library of Congress Cataloging-in-Publication Data

Levis, Larry.
   The gazer within / Larry Levis ; edited by James Marshall,
Andrew Miller, and John Venable ; with the assistance of
Mary Flinn
       p.   cm. — (Poets on poetry)
   ISBN 0-472-09718-0 (alk. paper) —
   ISBN 0-472-06718-4 (pbk. : alk. paper)
   1. Levis, Larry.   2. Poets, American—20th century—
Biography.   3. Poetry—Authorship.   4. Poetry.   I. Marshall,
James.   II. Miller, Andrews.   III. Venable, John.   IV. Title.
V. Series.
PS3562.E922 Z47   2000
811'.54—dc21
                                                    00-10490

*For all of Larry's students,
and for Nicholas*

Once, I thought even through this
I could go quietly as a star
turning over and over
in the deep truce of its light.
                              —"Fish"

But some things are not possible on the earth.
And that is why people make poems about the
     dead.
And the dead watch over them, until they are
     finished.
          —"For Zbigniew Herbert, Summer, 1971,
                              Los Angeles"

Once, I marched & linked arms with other
     exiles who wished to end a war, & . . .
Sometimes, walking in that crowd, I became the
     crowd, & for that moment, it felt
Like entering the wide swirl & vortex of history.
                    —"Caravaggio: Swirl & Vortex"

Acknowledgments

We would like to acknowledge the following publications and thank them for permission to reprint material appearing in this collection:

"'Larry Levis': Autobiography" was first published in *Contemporary Authors Autobiography Series,* vol. 23 (Detroit: Gale Research, 1996), ©1996.

"On Philip Levine" is adapted from "Philip Levine," in *On the Poetry of Philip Levine: Stranger to Nothing,* ed. Christopher Buckley (Ann Arbor: University of Michigan Press, 1990), 337–43.

"Strange Days: Zbigniew Herbert in Los Angeles" was first published in *Antioch Review* 45, ©1987.

"Eden and My Generation" was first published in *Field* 26, ©1982.

"Oaxaca and the Politics of Looking" was published by Polaroid in the winter 1986 issue of *Close Up,* ©1986.

"Some Notes on the Gazer Within" was first published in *Field* 26, ©1982.

"So That: On Holub's 'Meeting Ezra Pound' " was first published in *Field* 49, ©1993.

"Some Notes on Grief and the Image" was first published by Beacon Press in *Of Solitude and Silence: Writings on Robert Bly,* edited by Richard Jones and Kate Daniels, ©1981.

"Mock Mockers after That" was first published in *Marlboro Review* (winter–spring 1997), edited by Ruth Anderson Barnett, ©1997.

The coda was originally published in the photo-essay "One Hundred American Seducers on Their Craft and Sullen Art," which appeared in the August 16, 1973, issue of *Rolling Stone,* ©1973.

Contents

Editors' Note

This book comprises much of the nonfiction prose Larry Levis wrote. Larry considered collecting his essays in the 1980s, but a Fulbright fellowship to Yugoslavia and a windfall of new poems caused him to shelve the project indefinitely, and he had not completed it at the time of his death in May 1996. Our task has been to select the pieces most representative and revealing of his interests as a poet and skills as a critic. The book that results is both incisive and unified, for Larry's critical concerns rarely diverge from the poetic. Much as Yeats wrote the arguments of certain of his poems before committing them to verse, Larry turned to the essay to exercise the ideas that were to preoccupy, especially, his last four volumes of poems. Taken as a whole, *The Gazer Within* offers as much insight into his own poetry as into the subjects of its component meditations.

The order of the essays reflects the creative progression that started with *The Dollmaker's Ghost* (published in its first edition in 1981) and continued through *Elegy* (published posthumously in 1997) and was guided by three questions in particular: Where and through what processes does the poet acquire his vision of the self? What responsibilities and dangers does the poet face when gazing within his consciousness thus dually inflected by the poet's apprehension of *place,* of the basic fact of his location in a particular landscape, and by the unfolding of his essential experiences there? Finally, how does this consciousness of responsibility and danger affect the poet's ability to cope within the historical present, or with what Wallace Stevens calls the "pressure of reality?" Here the reader may observe Larry's progression through these questions in a variety of contexts, seeking to extend his vision out into a world that "built, almost simultaneously, the tract home, the atomic bomb, and the Dixie cup." It is the scrupulous abjection of the gazer that makes possible a belated, radical innocence in the world.

Concerns of balance and scope led to a difficult decision to omit or edit several works, among them interviews, book reviews, occasional pieces, and a substantial consideration of the contemporary war lyric as exemplified in the work of Zbigniew Herbert and Carolyn Forché. A complete listing of the uncollected prose is included at the end of this volume.

We could not have accomplished this task without the input and support of Sheila Brady, Greg Donovan, Anne Glenn, T. R. Hummer, Leslie Kelen, Michael Keller, Philip Levine, Nicholas Levis, Greg Pendergast, David St. John, Marcia Southwick, David Wojahn, Charles Wright, the Virginia Commonwealth University Department of English, and the *New Virginia Review*. For her tireless assistance and resources we thank Mary Flinn. We would also like to take this opportunity to thank Mark Bibbins, Mark Jarman, and David Lehman for advice and effort in preparing the manuscript for publication. We owe each of you a debt of gratitude.

Foreword

David St. John

Of the poets of his generation, Larry Levis spoke most powerfully of what it means to be a poet at this historical moment. With the same majesty he brought to his poetry, Larry Levis engaged his readers with the most subtle and disturbing questions of the self to be found in the prose—essays, reviews, or interviews—of any contemporary American poet. Broadly international in his scope and deeply personal in his reflections, he addressed poetic concerns that are both immediate and timeless. For many of us who struggle with these issues, Levis's prose on poetry stands as some of the most capacious to be found since Rilke's famous letters to the young poet.

Larry Levis's understanding of the dilemmas facing modern writers has always amazed me. Whether discussing Zbigniew Herbert or the idea of Eden in the work of his contemporaries, he brought to bear the admirable range of his own reading experience and coupled it with his casual yet incisive style. His eclectic tastes, his generosity of spirit, and his compassionate (and often startling) readings of other poets combine to make this collection of his prose a landmark event.

In talking about himself, as in the autobiographical essay that begins this collection, Larry Levis could be more surprising, candid, self-effacing, and dramatic in thirty pages than any dozen writers' memoirs that have assailed us in recent years. Perhaps that's because we can always feel the discretion and precision, as well as the tremendous force, of Levis's intelligence at work. He loved to recall—as he does in this essay, with great passion—his own coming to poetry and, of course, the beginnings of his lifelong friendship with his first teacher at California State University, Fresno, the poet Philip Levine.

As he makes clear in his essay on Levine, it was to be the defining friendship of his life.

As a poet who came of age in the sixties, Levis often considered his own work (as well as the work of other poets) in a political context. I think this must be understood not as a didactic impulse in his writing and thinking, but as a humanitarian urgency. Even so, Levis also had something of the aesthete about him; he never lost his love of Baudelaire and the French Symbolists. He insisted upon the power of art and beauty, as rendered in the context of human experience (often human pain and suffering); nor did he overlook the drive of individual desire and aspiration. For Levis, "culture" was never abstract; it always began and ended in a particular person.

In reading again these long-familiar essays, I was struck by their acute and disarming critical thinking. I was also stunned to realize how filled with awe, even an exceptional innocence, these pieces remain. Levis never resorts to cynicism and its innately superior position. Think how rare that is. Above all else, it is this aspect of his work that reveals most clearly his respect for other poets and for the art and act of poetry.

Levis's belief in the power of language is something we recognize again and again in his poetry. This virtue makes itself felt throughout his prose as well. His ear for speech and nuance of character (as revealed in that speech) is often surprising (again, witness the essay on Levine). Even when he is talking about himself (or his poetry) his mastery of tone takes hold. There is often a wry, sardonic edge to these pieces that reminds me that Larry Levis was indeed the single funniest person I have ever known. From his wicked, drop-dead imitations of Mick Jagger to his dry, deadpan anecdotes of literary and academic life, he often had his friends falling off their chairs. This capacity is hinted at in his autobiography's invocations—which are imitations—of the wicked and hilarious talk of the farmworkers he grew up with. One can only wish he had left us more of this dimension of his darkly consoling humor.

These essays remind us of the importance of the physical world—of place, of landscape—in Levis's poetry and in his thinking about poetry. His deep empathy with the landscapes he moved through is something we know well from his poetry;

such empathy is dramatically displayed in this collection as well, perhaps especially in his evocations of his native California and in his essay on Oaxaca. For Levis, the authentic experience of any landscape was—necessarily—also an experience of one's own humanity. Therefore, his engagement with "place" is as passionate as his engagement with the figures of that place. So too does the place reflect and refract those many aspects of the self that Levis lovingly held up to the light of language in both these essays and his poetry.

What *The Gazer Within* makes clear is Larry Levis's devotion to the art of poetry and his love of the many pleasures of thought. He granted himself the luxury of observing the world in all of its richness. With none of the presumptions or pretensions of lesser writers and with a generosity lacking in many, Larry Levis has written the most impassioned prose on poetry of any of his contemporaries.

"Larry Levis": Autobiography

First Impression

It isn't dramatic or fashionable to begin with being born, but for me it was an important event. According to the diary of my grandmother, in which little is noted except a half century or more of weather, I was born at 3:00 A.M. in a rainstorm on the last day of September 1946. When I was twelve, driving a tractor, furrowing out a vineyard of muscats for my father one day, I was for some reason immediately impressed by how lucky I was to have been born at all, especially to be born as a human being rather than, as I wrote later in a poem, "a horse, or a gnat." I was easily impressed, I guess, but the moment was full of wonder.

First Confession

My mother, whose maiden name was Carol Clement Mayo, was Irish. I was raised as a Catholic, which is to say, raised to believe that such terms as *mystery, spirit,* and the *Holy Ghost* were real presences rather than abstractions. To be raised as a Catholic is to grow up feeling guilty for something but not to know quite what it is. At seven, like other children, I went to my First Confession so that I could receive, afterward, my First Communion. Like other children, I had to make up sins on the way to my First Confession, mostly venial sins, like lying or having "bad thoughts." I had made up about ten little sins, but I felt I ought to confess to at least one big Mortal Sin,

From *Contemporary Authors Autobiography Series,* ed. Joyce Nakamura, vol. 23 (Detroit: Gale Research, 1996), 181–92.

just to get it down somehow, from the start. A mortal sin was serious business. If you didn't confess, do penance, and gain absolution by Communion, you would go straight to hell in the next life without a lawyer made of air at your side, without even an arraignment or hearing. I looked at the list of the ten mortal sins and realized right away that I didn't qualify as a transgressor for nine of them. The only one left was a word I didn't understand, and so I thought that must be the sin that I had committed, the one that applied to me. And so, at the age of seven, after confessing my little, imaginary venial sins, I confessed to adultery, I did it in a casual, offhand way, "And uh . . . I committed adultery," I said. The priest stopped mumbling to himself in Latin. There was, in the shadowy, screened, small space of the confessional where I knelt, a silence, a pause. I could tell I'd made some sort of impression. He asked, "How many times, my son?" "Just once," I replied. And then he asked, "How *old* are you?" "I'm seven, Father," I answered. And so he then explained what adultery was. And after he had finished, I said, "Oh no. I haven't done *that!*" And so it must have been something else that I had done that I wished to atone for, though I didn't know what it was. I still don't. But Catholicism works its shrewd miracle in the seven-year-old psyche, or soul, before the mind can question it.

You feel guilty for something or other you've done or just thought about doing, and you can't remember what it was or know what it was, and it keeps you in line, for a while at least, off the streets and out of trouble. Sometimes it works for ages. What else could have coerced peasants to lug huge stones up a hill for a cathedral except a hope to atone for the only sin they had all committed, the sin of being mortal, of being born and knowing they were flesh, and flesh must die. They didn't do it out of *altruism*. It doesn't exist. I was eight or nine when I realized this. I was loitering around by my father's abandoned chicken shed, a long, low building that still smelled vaguely of chicken dung. I was trying to pray without any self-interest. I couldn't do it. St. Augustine knew this long before I did.

Besides, it was a world with a chicken shed in it. My father once had a going egg business. He hated it. He hated chickens, and he finally grew to despise even their eggs. "What was the happiest day of your life?" I once asked him. "The day I got out of the chicken business," he answered; there was more to the world than belief, or disbelief.

I wasn't religious and never have been. The Mass was in Latin, and the incomprehensible sound of it had a beauty, but going to Mass always bored me. It seemed like a complete waste of time. And catechism classes were worse. The nuns longed for any opportunity to punish us. They watched as if we were a group of suspects the police had rounded up. They knew we were guilty of something.

The Catholic Church understood Freud's concept of the superego centuries before he articulated it in 1940. The cathedral on a hill is its palpable and visible representation, or, in Freud's simile, the superego is "like a garrison above a captured town." In the case of the church, it is a garrison so effective that it doesn't even need soldiers. Its windows are beautiful. Its frescoes and painting and sculptures, depicting absence in enormous detail, are priceless. It enabled Dante to imagine hell, and it was at least the stepmother to a ninety-year period of Italian art, a period of corruption, betrayal, incest, assassination, intrigue, and unsurpassable art. The church knew beauty and evil were sleeping together, and gave both allowances to do it. Two thousand years of stolid, industrious virtue and Swiss peace perfected the cuckoo clock and the dairy cow. I suspect the Swiss dairyman had a good deal of placid self-esteem. Michelangelo hated himself. And a later figure, Caravaggio, was mean-tempered, an inadvertent murderer whose self-portrait, as Goliath, is full of self-contempt and despair.

In the Age of Therapy, First Confessions could be seen as a ritualized form of child abuse, psychological in method, permanent in effect. But you can't take the Vatican to court. The painting on the chapel's ceiling doesn't respond to a summons and is tricky evidence.

In my case, I would lie awake as a child, full of vague yearnings which were sexual, which I did not know were entirely normal. I was never abused nor molested nor violated as a child. I simply felt that I *was* a violation, that I was guilty of being alive.

But if it was a violation, it was a pleasure. Besides, how guilty can anyone feel, at seven or eight? I was a boy like other boys. I didn't rebel against guilt, I forgot about it.

Before I was born, a priest drowned in our swimming pool. He had a weak heart and dove into cold, fresh water. My mother came out with a tray of glasses and ice tea and saw him bobbing there. She felt terrible about it. I always thought it was amazing. Priests were full of a mysterious divinity. They had a little bit of God in them. They weren't supposed to die like other people. This one was a young priest from Kingsburg. His lungs were full of water. His body was heavy. My mother pulled him out and tried to revive him with artificial respiration, but of course it didn't work. I always imagined him floating face down in a robe and vestments, dressed for saying the Mass, and asked my mother about it once when I was still a child. "No, silly," she said, "he had on bathing trunks." God died in his bathing trunks, I thought then, for priests were the form He took on earth. Did He really die, I wondered, or did He just do it to show that he could do it too, flick *It* into the pool water like a fourth of July sparkler burning too close to the hand? He did a lot of things just for effect, I thought: Yosemite National Park, for example.

Thinking about God made me tired. I had trouble believing in everlasting life. What did it look like? It seemed more likely that one just died in the end, and that was that, I had begun to think. If the spirit rose off you like a mist, so what? I'd hunted quail in thick ground fog that broke up and parted like mist when the sun burned it off. I hunted without a dog and entirely by intuition and always found quail. My senses grew alive and sharp when I hunted. The quail would burst up around me. I had a twenty-gauge shotgun and would usually bring down four or five by the time I'd finished. It felt real. It was pointless to think about God. Heaven made me feel tired, baffled, resigned, sad as when someone tells you a lie, and you know it's a lie, and wonder why he had to do so. When I cleaned the quail they were still warm inside. Their feathers gave off a pungent, wild smell that was like nothing else. I neglected to cut their feet off; it didn't seem important. My mother hated cooking them. I'd have to break the thin gray sticks of their legs off before she was willing to.

4

People now confess to all kinds of things, in public, on television. I have a feeling they too make up the things they confess to, just as we did, at seven. But they enjoy it, they like confessing to things. If they've done something that can still shock an audience, they even get paid for it, or make money later by confessing it in a book. They are absolved of their sins by the show's ratings and by book sales. We were supposed to feel embarrassment, shame, and contrition over what we had done. We were just kids. But we tried. We'd shut our eyes and concentrate and try to feel each one of those things. We couldn't, and we would feel sorry when we couldn't. They should have paid us money for it.

"But God comes to see without a bell."

The Ranch

Everyone who lived there or worked there always referred to it as, simply, "the ranch." My mother, who is eighty-four now, still lives in the old white brick-and-frame two-story house attached to a weathered, frame windmill tower where there hasn't been a windmill for years. A long gravel driveway lined with orange and olive and tangerine and cypress and palm trees leads up to it, and the gravel looks almost white in the moonlight. A family of owls nests in the spreading—and I was almost about to say "ancient"—limbs of some kind of pine above the roof, and anyone sleeping upstairs can be awakened by their shrieks and screeching at night as they hunt or come back with some drained field mouse to feed to their young. Except for that it is so quiet at night you hear only the quiet if you've been away and lived in a city and come back. In the morning now I am awakened by the sound of a rake over gravel because Johnny Dominguez, who is retired from work on the ranch, still rakes leaves and pine needles from the gravel each morning, either out of habit or because he promised my father he would do so after my father died whether there were leaves or anything to rake there or not. When there are no leaves, he rakes the gravel.

I was born in 1946 in a place that seemed to exist, the fields and vineyards and even the sky over it all, in some motionless and unchanging moment. From the upstairs bedroom window, the rows of vineyards run on to a horizon of foothills, and it has the quiet and proportion of a landscape van Gogh painted once, nothing at all like *Starry Night,* which changed painting forever perhaps, but the ordered fields he clung to as he painted as if he was clinging to sanity itself before him. My California, the vineyards and orchards on the east side of the San Joaquin Valley, have remained unviolated, for the most part, by developers and suburbs. The land looks as if nothing has changed there. But that isn't so.

The land was settled, and then it was unsettled. My father and other small farmers, in order to keep up economically with a market that demanded earlier and earlier varieties of fruit, especially peaches and plums, tore out old orchards of Reynosa and late Elberta peaches and orchards of late plums and supplanted them with new varieties developed by University of California, Davis, that they could harvest in late May and early June and send on refrigerated boxcars to markets in the East. The new varieties, especially peaches with unsigned, authorless, corporate names like Early May Golds or whatever, were attractive to shoppers in supermarkets: they had size, texture, and lots of color, and they were in the markets by late spring. The new varieties of peaches had no flavor and no sweetness. Their flesh was tough instead of ripe and tender. They were the product of modern farming, which had become a product of modern business. And small farmers as well, as Wendell Berry has pointed out in *The Unsettling of America,* a brilliant and too often ignored book, were encouraged to think of themselves as businessmen, as participants in agribusiness as completely as large corporate farmers participated in it. The orchards and vineyards dozed on in their blankets of chemicals, everything from sulfur and malathion to DDT and parathion. As an example of what happened to the land in the mid–twentieth century, parathion is interesting: after parathion was sprayed on an orchard, signs were posted along its borders, warning everyone to stay out of it for a week because, theoretically at least, the chemical on unprotected skin could affect the nerve endings and, in dosages large enough, could even paralyze someone who happened to take an innocent stroll through the trees.

The trouble with all this is that small farmers were not corporate business managers. They were small farmers. They took pride in what they did. Agribusiness and modern marketing had little to do with them, but they had to survive and go along with what was called "progress" in those days even when they knew it was someone's idea of a slick hustle.

Laughing in Spanish

That land! It was a kind of paradise preserved, held intact, by the toxic perfume of malathion and sulfur, insecticide sprays, fertilizers, and by the people who worked on it, who were Mexican if they were older, Chicano if younger, who spoke Spanish mostly, and who were underpaid. Many of them lived in poverty and the intermittent misery of unemployment. It's wrong to characterize a people, but in an interview, late in his life, Cesar Chavez gestured toward a family of farmworkers sitting under a tree after lunch and said to the journalist next to him, "You see? They are so . . . innocent." I knew exactly what he meant.

"They" were not a "they" to me. They were men I worked with in orchards and vineyards. Their names, which deserve to be mentioned and which won't be unless I do it, were Angel and John Dominguez, Tea, Ignacio Calderon, Ediesto and Jaime Huerta, Coronado, Fermín, and the older man who had beautiful manners and who rarely spoke and who ate his lunch alone, apart from the others, whom they called Señor Solo.

I worked with them regularly, season after season on the ranch, and they teased me endlessly with great affection. They called me by their chosen nickname for me, Cowboy, the accent falling on the last instead of the first syllable, Cow*boy*. I felt honored to work beside them, because I *was* only a boy, and an Anglo boy at that, and the son of the *patron,* my father. They would have found the term *Hispanic* imprecise and puzzling and amusing, and the new word, *Chicano,* had a political hue to it and referred to the young. As far as they were concerned, they were Mexicans. Toward women and children they were gallant and infinitely considerate. They talked and sang in a Spanish that seemed to me full of mysterious grace and almost courtly manners which they blended with put-downs in slang to hilarious effect: "Con su permiso, Jaime, su cafe no vale tres chingaderas. Pero muchisima gracias, sin embargo." Which is to say: "With your permission, Jimmy, your coffee is not worth three motherfuckers. But I thank you for it with an infinite gratitude nonetheless." To which Jaime, holding his thermos of coffee, might reply, though I translate it: "Though I have so far refrained from mentioning it because it was a task requiring no courage and performed as an act of simple decency and out of sanitary considerations, it has occurred to me that I did, however inadvertently, save your life the other day. I killed a shit-eating dog." And they would go on: "Spoken thanks, in that case, would be a form of dishonor. And therefore my gratitude shall take the material form of five million frozen turds paid to you in installments the day after each Christmas for as long as I live, Don Pínche."

Fermín made it into an art, almost. He had been well educated somewhere, and was articulate in Spanish and English, but had got into trouble of some kind either here or in Mexico and so slipped into the anonymity and oblivion of migrant labor camps. Once, pretending to be a kind of deposed grandee, he began his elaborate put-down in this manner:

Most of us working patiently alongside you today, *Querido Flaco,* though we did not enjoy it nor do we expect any payment for laboring overtime, did try, last night, out of our kind consideration for your happiness, to instruct your *novia* in the art of love. I will say she began to respond with more and more enthusiasm, but with only a slight improvement in skill. She is, however, an eager student whose attention and stamina never wavered even after she had exhausted her teachers, who remain—even if one of them said, later, that "it was like trying to teach a stick to fly"—your loyal and generous friends. I think, *Kamikajisimo,* I should mention that at one point in the night, brushing out her *pendeja,* she compared your *falo,* you know, your *pleaser,* to a communion wafer in church, and said that the wafer, the host, stayed harder longer as it melted in her mouth in a matter of seconds than your *pene* ever has, wherever she has found it. But as for what she might confess next time before she takes Communion, I wouldn't worry too much. One must feel some contrition for one's sins in order to confess them, and what she feels is far from even the remotest forms of regret. As Father Cabrón explained it to me when I asked about it, her sensual anticipation of further instruction as well as her almost continual state of expectant sexual arousal these days are in reality not feelings at all, but sensations. In such a condition, he said, clear thinking is impossible for her, just as it has always been.

Apparently it mattered little to Fermín that Kijima was almost sixty, had emigrated from Okinawa, spoke nothing but Japanese, and had never had a girlfriend or even a friend, as far as anyone knew, except for a half-blind mottled dog that slept in the shade under someone's car or pickup most of the afternoon.

Everyone had laughed, of course. And Kijima smiled with pleasure and complete incomprehension. But then the oldest men there, at first Angel Dominguez, and then Tea, told Fermín that the joke was unkind, that it amounted to no more than the pointless humiliation of an old man, even if that man did not understand a word of it, and that he, Fermín, should feel ashamed and should apologize to Kijima even if he could not understand the apology either. We worked on, picking peaches, in silence after this, for most of us had laughed. No one had ever contradicted the judgment of Angel or Tea, and no one did so now. Finally, after about an hour, Fermín went up to Kijima and apologized for telling the joke. Kijima bowed and smiled, not understanding a word. And then, slowly, one by one, everyone working in the trees would come down from his ladder and go up to Kijima where he was working and apologize, in Spanish, mostly. In my case, in English. Kijima had no idea what we were saying to him, but he bowed to each of us and smiled anyway.

"You see? They are so innocent," said Chavez. They had dignity as well. The slow ritual under the trees by which each of us gave back to Kijima the dignity we had swiped from him by laughing was part of the innocence of that world. It is not extinct, that innocence, even now. It exists on the outskirts of small towns like Parlier and Del Rey, places where "executives would never want to tamper." It would make it easier for us to live, I guess, if it were extinct, because then there would be nothing to remind us of how much of it had disappeared, nothing to disgrace us by the sudden austere appearance of dignity in the voices of two old men laboring in the trees, working in a slow but unwavering rhythm, as if there was in it a pride to maintain, in each numberless and quiet twist of their wrists something that can no longer be understood, some *dignidad,* something completely unmarketable in the world.

I idealize them, of course. They would be puzzled by my praise of them. And tease me about it. One day after work Ignacio said, "Hey, Cowboy, it's payday. You wanna come with me to Parlier? I know this place where they have *putas.* I like the big ones myself, the ones with real long legs, but they got some little tiny ones too, if you want. Come with me." I was maybe twelve at the time. "I can't," I said. "My mom won't let me." But after a few seconds had passed, I asked, "How much are the little tiny ones?" And they all howled with laughter. I'm sure I idealize them. But oblivion has no right to claim them without my respect, without their names written down, here and elsewhere.

My Parents and One Good Line I Wrote at Sixteen

Their morals were Victorian and their politics were conservative. They were children of the Depression and wary of most social change. They were also children of the Cold War and its successful propaganda, which made them fear communism and the labor union Chavez organized. They belonged to the Skeleton Club and would go dancing there in a large hall with other farm families, but they remained suspicious of the Grange, which they thought leaned toward socialism.

Once, while I was working with Tea in a vineyard of muscats, I made some complaint about my father. Tea felt I was wrong and hastened to correct me. "No," he said, "su padre tiene dignidad." I asked him what things made up *dignidad.* "Corazón," he replied, and then smiled, "Corazón y cojónes." Heart and balls. Courage, in other words. My father certainly had that. Once, as I was riding with him in his pickup along a two-lane country road surrounded by vineyards, we came upon a small group of men in the middle of the road, a circle with two men inside it. They were young men, farm laborers, Mexicans, and one held a grape-cutting knife with a sharpened blade in his hand, his fore and index finger on either side of the curved point so that it could slash like a razor. The other man may have had a knife as well, but all I saw was a coat rolled around one arm to ward off the other's blade. My father abruptly stopped the truck, told me to stay in it, got out and walked without any hesitation right into the middle of the circle, between the two men, shoving each one roughly back and away from the other, and then demanded that the one holding it give him the knife. The man did so, an expression of surprise or consternation on his face. My father got back in the truck but didn't say anything about it. We drove on and had coffee in a little lunch counter in Parlier where other farmers usually gathered in the late morning to kid each other and complain about poor prices, poor crops. My father didn't mention the fight even then, when someone asked him what he'd done that morning. I didn't either. They were ranchers, farmers, and they looked like it in their rumpled work clothes and hats with soiled brims and stained hat bands. I didn't say anything there unless one of them asked me a question.

When we got back to the house, my father did what he always did. He ate a light lunch, went into the living room to rest for a half hour or so before going back to work, and listened to classical music or opera while he lay on the couch. He was neither articulate nor talkative. Like Robert Lowell's portrait of Colonel Shaw, my father seemed "to wince at pleasure / and suffocate for privacy." I asked him once if he believed in God. He said he did. I asked him if that guaranteed everyone some kind of eternal life. He said he didn't see how it could and that such a thing seemed impossible whenever he had thought about it.

He was reserved, but not dour. He could always make my mother laugh with some joke or other, and did so almost daily. By the time I was in high school, my sisters and my brother were off in college, and I was the only child still living with my parents. It was clear to me, especially as they grew older, that the two of them really loved each other, even delighted each other. They were an example of something, especially to me.

I've been married three times and divorced three times. But I did at least once witness a marriage that was happy, one that lasted. In my case, I could say, with Yeats, that one must make a choice between one's art and one's life. Once or twice, I have done that, I suppose. But it seems to me I had to choose between one kind of life or another kind of life. Yeats makes the choice sound rather grand and heroic and heartbreaking enough, for everyone involved. But to actually split up with someone because you believe it is a sacrifice for Art is, it seems to me, a kind of semiprecious delusion, as Yeats suggests as he concludes his poem.

In his whole life, my father wrote only two letters to me. Both began "How's tricks?" My father felt about as comfortable with writing as someone might who holds a poisonous snake on the end of a stick, or, on these occasions, at the end of a pencil. But my father was full of contradictions, as most people are. If he wasn't terribly talkative, the things he did say mattered. And I might as well continue with the aforementioned snake. My family had a cabin in the Sierras at Shaver Lake, and, one afternoon, hiking with my brother and my sisters, all of them far older than I, I saw, or at least I thought I saw, a rattlesnake resting under a manzanita bush, and I shouted and screamed. We all raced back to the shore of the lake where our boat was tied and where my father and mother were preparing a picnic. My brother and my sisters, by the time we got there, had ceased to believe that I had seen a snake at all, and, I confess, I was beginning to disbelieve it myself. It might have been the way the sun was shining on the manzanita limbs and the ground beneath them. But they kept teasing me, until I felt humiliated and began crying. I was maybe seven or so at the time and kept insisting to my father that there really was a snake at the top of the path above us. I was simply afraid of rattlesnakes, and I was a child, and at that moment I suspected that I had imagined seeing one when nothing was there. My father turned and went up the path and then, a few minutes later, came back. They were still teasing me and I was still crying and still angry at them and at myself, and, by then, I was certain I had only imagined the snake. My brother looked at my father and said, sarcastically, "Well, what about it? Was there a snake up there?" I waited for my father to confirm everyone's suspicion that I was lying about the whole thing. A summer of endless teasing and humiliation stretched before me. And then my father said the most marvelous thing, which I was sure, even then, was a lie. He said, "Yeah, there was a snake up there. I saw it." My father lied for me! He could see I was miserable and he lied for me. I knew it and he knew it. If the snake had existed, how would he have known where to look for it? Why would it still be there if he had known?

Years later, I would still remember the incident. I do not know whether my father had an imagination or not. He did not allow it to show, if he did. But he certainly defended the imagination, or my imagination, by lying for me that day. And he saved me from ridicule.

As a child, I drew all the time, and by the age of twelve I was drawing nudes in school when I was bored. One day my mother found a kind of obscene anatomical sketch of a naked woman in my pants pocket and showed it to my father later in the day. My father was outraged. "Did you draw this?" he asked me. I couldn't answer, but my face told him all he needed to know. "I'm disgusted with you," he said.

Love and shame. Imagination had its consequences. His remark had expelled me from the paradise of his affection. I no longer thought of myself or was capable of thinking of myself as categorically good. As in "a good boy." Of course my father forgave me and meant nothing final by what he had said. But it had changed things. It had changed my relationship to him and changed the way I saw myself. My sketch mocked the woman in it, who was fat, naked, with huge breasts and thighs, and flourishing pubic hair. And my father had only contempt for the kind of disrespect in it. The drawing meant nothing much to me. I was twelve. I was interested in sex. And afraid of sex. I had to imagine a naked body I could not have in the flesh. But the sketch changed things. I wasn't a good boy after that. I did not have to try to be a good boy, especially, because I wasn't one. My father had as much as said so.

My father couldn't have prepared me better for my life as a poet if he had tried, if he had read Homer to me every night, for in two years I would take up smoking, out of a sort of rebellion, and at the age of fifteen I was the only kid for miles around who owned an album by Bob Dylan, and I was certainly the only kid in my high school who read poetry, who loved T. S. Eliot mostly, who read Frost and then Stevens. Four years later, when I was sixteen, I decided, one night, to try to write a poem. When I was finished I turned out the light. I told myself that if the poem had one good line in it I would try to be a poet. And then I thought, no, you can't say "try." You will either be a poet, and become a better and better one, or you will not be a poet. The next morning I woke and looked at what I'd written. It was awful. I knew it was awful. But it had one good line. One. All the important decisions in my life were made in that moment.

My father died at seventy-eight of a combination of Parkinson's, a series of small strokes, and old age. After the largely unconvincing Catholic service, my family went back to the ranch, and I held the box with his "ashes" in it. It was heavier than the term "ashes" implies. His remains were bits of whitened bone mostly, and, with my family around me, I strewed them into a furrow in an orchard of Elberta peaches he was proud of. No one mentioned God or Heaven or anything like that. It would have been tasteless somehow. No one said anything except my mother, who said "He's home." We all walked back to the house.

My mother's hair is snow white. It has been for years. She never moved from the ranch after my father died, and she is still strong and plucky. She needs a knee operation which she has no interest in getting. She will sometimes tell me that certain things in my poems didn't happen the way I said they did, that I had made up things and made them sound like facts. I remembered them, or remembered them told to me, as I wrote them. But perhaps she's right. Anecdotes don't reveal her. She has always been more a presence in my life, someone forgiving, sympathetic beyond what I sometimes deserved, loving, irreplaceable. When I go to the ranch now to see her, she holds my arm as we go up the steps. This step. Then the next.

Blame and accusation fill the best-selling memoirs of our time. The parents are usually indicted for just about every kind of neglect, abuse, and failure. I couldn't blame mine for anything, not even my father's remark, which was mild enough as such things go with parents and children. If I took it seriously enough for it to liberate me in some way, I guess I can only blame my shrewd, calculating unconscious for that. For my father and mother, I feel only gratitude. They always helped me. They didn't see how I'd ever make a living as a poet, and they worried, and they always helped me.

High School

I was reading Yeats. I had my own copy passed down by my sister Sheila, who has always encouraged me. I was glad to have my own book because our high school librarian had taken Yeats's poems out of the stacks. One day he had surprised two girls laughing over "Leda and the Swan," which their teachers had recommended they read. I don't know why he removed it except that the high school was in the country, in a farming community. Sex with swans is not funny in a farming community, I guess. Sex with animals period is not funny, I suppose our librarian believed. Yeats was banned. Yeats was obscene. That was that.

One of the girls (they *were* girls, then) said, "She did it with a *swan*? She was pregnant and told everyone a *swan* knocked her up? Yeah right." The girl's name was Liz. I had an unspoken crush on her for four years. I had acne. I was shy around girls, though I desired them. I wasn't much good at football and only mediocre as a swimmer. I had the world's slowest car, a 1957 four-door Plymouth Plaza with a push-button transmission and a flathead six engine. I had been on horses that were faster, both in acceleration and top-end speed. I tried to mask my insecurity by seeming worldly and indifferent, a cynical, adolescent clown. I didn't "get laid," as they put it then, though I wanted to. Sex in high school was less common in the mid-sixties than it became later, although some couples who were "going together" had achieved that important, decently human pleasure. In my senior year, I took Liz home from some class party or other. She kissed me goodnight, sweetly but seriously. If she had merely intended it as therapy, it worked far better than weeks of counseling. When I saw her twenty years later at a reunion, she had become a vice president of some corporation in Oregon and a marathon runner. She was still beautiful. They had all grown up, Liz, Cathy, Sharon, but they were all still beautiful, I thought, and they were now far more interesting. Cathy asked me about a book by the poet Sharon Olds because I'd written something for the jacket copy. I was amazed. I thought she lived in the untroubled waters of the Beautiful and had no need of poetry. My innocence was mostly ignorance, I thought then, after we had spoken.

Jeff Riehl was my best friend in those years, and Frank Anderson and Wayne Ota were close friends. I was lucky to know them. No one could have had better company than theirs. They were intelligent and funny. We could talk about anything together, no matter how foolish it was. They knew I was interested in poetry, and they didn't ridicule me for it, or ask what I'd do with it in the future, or how I would make a living. No time in my life was as emotionally awkward and difficult as adolescence and high school. I felt ridiculous for a year and a half before meeting them and becoming friends. There's nothing corny or sentimental about remembering them and how they interrupted my useless loneliness and useless self-pity, both of which are ways vanity disguises itself.

By 1965, some of the boys in my high school would go off to Vietnam, some would die there. The young woman who did it with the swan created tragedy. The swan went back to being just a swan, after he did it with her, and no one could find him among the innumerable others. The librarian had taught Latin. I don't know what became of him or if he's still alive. But he looked ageless, fifty or more with the face of a boy. Easily embarrassed. So much of the world seemed obscene to him then, when it was not, especially.

Hearts and Minds

As the years went on, it was the Vietnam War that became obscene. My friend Ed Zamora died in Vietnam. He was Hispanic or Chicano or simply of Mexican origin, however you prefer to say it, and he had dropped out of Reedley Junior

College because he couldn't afford college and had to go to work, and the draft picked him up. He died and I'm alive. I don't understand it. The injustice of it, the random, unpatternable thing life was, and is, feels like guilt, at first, and then matures (though the verb is obscene in the context) into sorrow. I lived, he didn't. Helen is brushing her hair. Troy is burning. Robert McNamara wept last night on television. It took him thirty years, but he did it, finally. The swan is squabbling over a crust of bread thrown by a child. The rented paddle boats make a splashy sound on the pond. The swan is just a swan.

Nineteen years after his death, I found my friend's name on the wall of the Vietnam Veteran's Memorial in Washington, D.C. I touched the carved letters of it with my fingers, then my face was wet with tears before I had any warning. Usually there is a second or two in which I have always been able to stop myself from crying. Those occasions are so infrequent. Our country teaches us not to weep. Not to grieve. It's almost a part of some curriculum of indifference, as if a new car could console us. I begin by thinking those years are part of my past, and the time swarms around me with its presences. Troy is a few acres of blurry grass, scattered stones, wind. The students I teach feel about as much for the Vietnam era as they do for the fall of Carthage, and they have a right to. But for most of my generation, that time lives on like an incurable affliction, like a tremor in the hand. I remember President Clinton at a news conference on television. He paused, listening to a difficult question. He listened but was thinking of something else, the famous "thousand-yard stare" on his face, I thought, the trait, the ineradicable if intermittently appearing, unasked-for tattoo of a generation.

A Misdiagnosis

I wasn't brave about it. At seventeen I simply knew that I did not want to go to Vietnam. I was afraid. I didn't want to die there. I didn't especially want to kill anyone, either. And I knew that if I didn't want to shoot a soldier in the Viet Cong, I probably would not. Being a communist did not seem a sufficient reason for killing someone. But he might have had several good reasons for killing me.

There were ways to avoid the draft, and the most expedient way was to stay in college. I heard of one young man who showed up at an induction center in Oakland with his father's deer rifle, a 30.06, I think it was. He told the officials there he wanted to go, he wanted badly to go to Vietnam, but, he said "I just want to kill 'em with my own gun, OK? Is that so hard to unnerstan', hunh?" They didn't take him.

It seemed only a matter of time before the war escalated enough so that they would draft students anyway. If the critics of Dan Quayle are correct, I wasn't brave either. I did what he did. I signed up for the California Air National Guard. My brother was in it, and somehow they found a place for me. I didn't last long. I may have the shortest military career on record: four days.

My balls kept me out of Vietnam. Not anything "ballsy" or rebellious that I did. No, I thank my balls, my testicles, for keeping me out of the Vietnam War. Let me explain: The year before I entered high school, my testicles, especially the right one, began to grow in size. I was scared and too embarrassed and ashamed to tell anyone about this. But after a few weeks, my scrotal sac was the size of a large grapefruit. Because of my Catholic upbringing, I thought it was my fault, that I had caused this to happen, that it was my punishment for the arousals and hard-ons of adolescence which happened with the frequency of thirst, punishment for the ways I fantasized about women, all women, younger, older, real, completely imagined, thin as pages in magazines or bosomy in the school desk beside mine. Our family doctor, Campbell Covington, also a Catholic, a man with a rich Carolina accent, said, "Wow, that thing's as big as a softball!" But it was only a hydrocele, a water sac around the right scrotal sac. It required a simple operation. When I asked him if it was because of something I'd done, he knew immediately what I was thinking and feeling. "No way," he said, "You haven't done anything. What's happened to your right nut, that's congenital, that was in the cards years ago. Now give me all that guilt you've been walking around with. Yeah, give it up. Leave it right here in the office." Portnoy knew what he was doing. I didn't, exactly. But after Dr. Covington talked to me, a vast weight lifted off my naive, provincial shoulders. I knew so little. I may as well have been raised by wolves in comparison to kids who had grown up in the town.

And so, six years later, at nineteen, I failed to pass the medical exam for induction into the California Air National Guard. I didn't know what I was doing there anyway. I had arrived late on my second day at the base, wearing my new, very dark green fatigues, and was told to race around the parade grounds. I couldn't find my "unit" there. I didn't even know who they were, and so I "fell out" with guys who looked like me, guys dressed in fatigues, and therefore formed the only one-person line in the formation, standing at the back. When the sergeant shouted "About Face!" everyone turned around, and I found myself leading them, a company of airplane mechanics. That was why they were dressed in fatigues. I was an Admin. Spec. 4; I could type. If I was ordered to go with the mechanics and work with them in the hangar, I could foresee the fiery wreckage of a jet. All because of me. I wandered back to the building and there was nothing for me to do, of course, and so I was told to get coffee for everyone, six cups of coffee. I was walking back when I spilled one of them, and my fatigues had a yard-long dark stain through the rest of the day. I felt as ridiculous as I looked. There was again nothing to do, so I was given a manual to read. One chapter was about what to do with top secret information in the event of imminent capture by the enemy. There was only one correct answer: "refer to your commanding officer."

Two days later they told me I was discharged from the guard. It was a medical discharge, and so, I guess, an honorable one. They said I would have to have exploratory surgery done because I had a tumor, maybe benign, maybe malignant, on my right ball. It had always been larger than a normal right ball, I thought then; even after the water sac operation. God was punishing me slowly and gradually, I thought, by giving me cancer of the right nut! I had tried to avoid dying in Vietnam by joining the jet jockeys local, only to find out I was dying anyway! And even if I wasn't, even if the tumor was found to be benign, I would then be transferred, according to military procedures, not back to the air national guard, but to the army and, probably, to Vietnam. Driving home that day, thinking I probably had cancer, I looked at the leaves on the passing trees, the sunlight on them. If leaves could sing, they were singing "I'm glad I'm not Larry."

But I didn't have a tumor. Dr. Covington said, "Those fools! That's just how I had to sew up the membrane after the operation. There's nothing there. No tumor. No cancer."

No Vietnam either. I registered late for my sophomore year and felt deliriously happy to be in school again. It was what I had longed to do. Not because I was an especially good student, but because I had already taken Philip Levine's workshop in my freshman year. He liked my work. I was a poet; I was going to become a much better one with any luck and a lot of work, and I had the great good fortune to have found a poet and genius for a teacher, one who has become a close and dear friend. I have written about Philip Levine elsewhere, but I feel certain that I would not have become a poet without being his student. He was simply amazing. His classes were better than any stand-up comedy act around, but his humor was serious. So was his passion for poetry. And he taught passionately. In many ways, he made my life and my poetry possible.

There were other poets at Fresno who were brilliant as well: Peter Everwine, Robert Mezey, Charles Hanzlicek. I absorbed all I could from them and learned as well from Jacque Ries, who taught comparative literature, and from Mort Bennett, who then owned the Cafe Midi, where I hung out and, for a brief time, worked, washing dishes.

If my right testicle kept me from being sent to the regular army and on to Vietnam, it's true that no one really escaped that war. In college I would join others and protest it. We would occupy buildings and block off streets. In a way, no one stayed out of Vietnam, because Vietnam grew immense enough to include us all. Protesting the war did not make most of us feel brave. Sometimes it at first seemed a kind of lark, closing off a street, sitting and joining arms there in it. When the buses pulled up and the riot police unspooled out of them in helmets and marched in formation toward us, what I felt was fear. I was scared. I think most of us were. The police had clubs. We didn't. They kept coming toward us to break us up or arrest us if we didn't leave. In those days, no one went peacefully. No one knew how to yet. It was something one had to learn. The current media caricatures of such protest make the demonstrators appear to be spoiled children at a naughty picnic turned bloody. It wasn't a joke. And it wasn't entertainment, either.

"Entertainment Is America's Passion," read a slogan on the back of a passing bus the other day. It was an ad for something or other. But for a few seconds, I thought it was a brilliant indictment of what the country had become. Fin de siècle America seems at times to be a nation of voyeurs. I'm not above it all by any means. I too watch television, though I don't own one anymore. I hadn't bothered to buy another one, for some reason. And I haven't had cable for years. Except for sports, news, public television, and a few movies, network TV shows are about as exciting as novocaine to relieve the pain of the sponsors' ads. I read late into the night, I read in bed, I read just about anything that interests me.

Demonstrations against the Vietnam War were confrontational. After the war, the country seemed to pass into history. It existed somewhere, but in a haze. You can't confront a haze. You can't block off a street all by yourself. When Noam Chomsky makes sense, there is a critic quick to characterize him as paranoid and include him with the paranoia of the right wing, as if all thought came to the same result. It doesn't. Power is hidden now. It views most of my students as a market and nothing more, and the media seems less independent than it did thirty years ago. In such a world, I was lucky. I became a poet because of a misdiagnosis. My balls did not want to go to war, it seems. I was in complete agreement with them.

An Ear

After Fresno, I went to Syracuse University for graduate study because the poet Donald Justice taught there. Justice had an *ear*, as we say in poetry. An ear doesn't sound like much in a world going deaf, but it may be as important in poetry as it is in music. Justice was not only a master of the music in poetry but also persuaded you that a certain kind of uncompromised intelligence, not just imagination, was called for if you wanted to try to make a thing that might last. When I later went to Iowa for a Ph.D., where he taught for years, I continued to learn from him. One night I was working late in my office, and he was too. I saw him going home in the corridor, dressed in a black overcoat. He was not especially well then. He had undergone bone or some sort of bone marrow surgery a few times for lingering if not chronic osteomyelitis. He was warning me about something or other—working too hard or staying up too late—I forget what it was exactly. In his black overcoat he seemed like César Vallejo, like a "presence" somehow, and as a poet I think he is at least as important as Vallejo, though completely different: for Justice, Reason itself was the mystery, an affliction which nothing could cure. It had a perverse beauty. Both poets, one a Peruvian Indian, the other the child of Georgia "crackers" who struggled against poverty, were acquainted with pain. At times, it kept intimate, inscrutable company with them. Vallejo's life was shorter, more tragic, but both poets had acquired a kind of bitterness, of the unacknowledged. The black overcoat is not insignificant in my portrait of him here. Justice once told me he had left Harvard in the winter of his freshman year because he couldn't afford an overcoat. The price of a coat does not seem like something that might determine one's fate, but this is so only if you have the money for one and the coat remains only a coat and doesn't stand for larger and more bewildering things you can do nothing about.

"Never forget what it meant to be truly poor," Pasolini once wrote. My teachers Philip Levine and Donald Justice did not forget what it meant. But they approached it far differently. I think of Levine, getting off the night shift at Chevy Gear and Axle at eighteen or nineteen, furious at how his life and the lives of those he loved was wasted by factory work, how his memory of it will become the great frankness and the vision of his poetry: "They feed they lion, and he comes," and, after he did come, the city that did not listen became an unlistening cinder; and of Justice, a child sitting on the rotting front porch of some general store in Florida, eating crackers and cheese, some phrase of Mozart running through is mind, becoming, in a key impossibly transposed—out of a changeling's childhood in which he must have just *assumed* he was the lost dauphin—the poetry he would write later: "The artist will have had his revenge for being made to wait, / A revenge not only necessary but right and clever— / Simply to leave him out of the scene, forever."

My respect for them never lessened or diminished. I became a teacher. Their example showed me that it was a serious thing to do. It is difficult to do it well, and worth it. There are poets I've met who disparage teaching, who do it only as a sort of chore, who think they're too good to teach. I don't know. I've worked in warehouses and packing sheds; I've driven trucks twelve hours a day and worked in fields and vineyards. I was not "too good" for that kind of work. But when I teach, I touch the past, the present, and the future, all in the same moment. Who is too good to do *that*? A poet who feels above such work might try to explain why to the guy coming off the swing shift in the grinding shed at Crucible Steel. He's had to inhale iron filings all evening because he can't make his quota while wearing the mask with the filter on it they give him. He can't even breathe if he wears that.

Luck

My first book of poems won the U.S. award of the International Poetry Forum and was published by University of Pittsburgh Press in 1972. My second, *The Afterlife,* was published in an edition of two hundred or so copies, beautifully printed by Kim Merker at the Windhover Press, but, as it won the Lamont Prize that year, the University of Iowa Press brought out a much larger edition. My third collection, *The Dollmaker's Ghost,* won the Open Competition of the National Poetry Series and was published by E. P. Dutton. My fourth and fifth collections, *Winter Stars* and *The Widening Spell of the Leaves,* were both published by University of Pittsburgh Press. I also wrote a book of prose, or stories as they may be, called *Black Freckles.* It was published by Peregrine Smith and sank like a stone in terms of sales or commentary. It freed me from any illusion that I might "try fiction."

I was awarded three NEA fellowships, a Guggenheim, and a Fulbright. I've taught at California State University, Los Angeles, Missouri, Iowa, Utah, and presently at Virginia Commonwealth University in Richmond.

I worked hard to write poetry. But I've had, I think, an enormous amount of luck as well.

Loves

I was married to the poet Marcia Southwick for almost ten years. We have a child, Nicholas, who is now seventeen. I was also married, at the age of twenty-two, to Barbara Campbell, and divorced four years later. In 1989, I married Mary Jane Hale, but we divorced a year later.

But the story of my love for them, and for other women, is part of my poetry and belongs there, not here.

And that is where it shall stay. After all, they are not memories.

Working Notes

I've mostly accounted here for my childhood, adolescence, and youth, perhaps because I can see it more clearly from this distance in time than I can see or remember in telling detail my adult life. But it seems to me that those early years were what determined everything, and what made me a poet. What kept me going as a poet were and are a lot of late nights, working until I get something, and then until I have it right, until the gray light of morning comes and I feel surprised that I've been working for so long. It never seems like work to me. It feels like pleasure. And even though I know it's toil, I keep that knowledge secret from some part of myself.

On Philip Levine

To attempt to be at all objective about my friend and my first teacher Philip Levine is impossible for me. For to have been a student of Levine's classes from the mid to late 1960s was to have a life, or what has turned out to be my life, *given* to me by another. And certainly then, at the age of seventeen, I *had* no life, or no passionate life animated by a purpose, and I was unaware that none might be possible.

It isn't enough to say that Levine was a brilliant young poet and teacher. Levine was amazing. His classes during those four years at Fresno State College were wonders, and they still suggest how much good someone might do in the world, even a world limited by the penitentiary-like architecture and stultifying sameness of a state college. For in any of these fifty-minute periods, there was more passion, sense, hilarity, and feeling filling that classroom than one could have found anywhere in 1964. If the class was difficult, if Levine refused to coddle students or protect the vanities of the lazy and mediocre from the truth about their work, if his criticism was harsh at times, all of this was justified and beautiful: justified because some students thought that an A could be had for repeating the clichés on greeting cards or that everything they did would be judged as mildly as finger painting in grade school; and it was beautiful because there poetry was given the respect it deserves and was never compromised to appease the culture surrounding it in the vast sleep of its suburbs, highways, and miles of dark packing sheds (all of

Adapted from "Philip Levine," in *On the Poetry of Philip Levine: Stranger to Nothing,* ed. Christopher Buckley (Ann Arbor: University of Michigan Press, 1990), 337–43.

which, I might add, if left without the intelligence and beauty of art, is in its mute entirety absolutely worthless).

But beneath the difficulty of the class, of studying and writing in traditional prosody, beneath the harshness of the criticism Levine gave to us, impartially and democratically, there was in the way he taught a humor and a talent for making the most self-conscious young students laugh at themselves and at their mistakes; by doing so, they could suddenly go beyond the uselessly narrow, brittle egos they had carried with them since junior high like a life savings in the wrong currency; that laughter woke them from the sleep of adolescence into something far larger. What was larger was the world of poetry, not only the study of it (passionate rather than impartial in Levine's readings of it), but also the possibility of writing it. If you could forget awhile your whining, hungry, sulking selves, Levine seemed to say to us, you could enter this larger world where the only president was Imagination. Levine made this the necessary world. And doing this made him unforgettable. It was a class like no other if only because it dared all of us in it to be considerably more alive than we wanted to be. In this sense it couldn't be compared to anything else I took there. In French 2B, for example, we recited a paragraph from *Eugénie Grandet* in French, and then once again, translated, in English. Nothing had changed in the format of French 2B since Charlemagne. My French professor was named Wesley Byrd. The one time I stopped in to see him during his office hours he was totally absorbed in plucking his eyebrows before a small hand mirror propped on his desk, and he did not pause in doing this even momentarily as he asked me to come in. "Professor Byrd," I asked, after a short interchange concerning the due date of a term paper, "after Rimbaud, did the alexandrine line disappear from French verse?" "Yes," he replied, snipping away, "gradually, it did." Then I asked, "What do you think of Rimbaud?" "Rimbaud?" he replied, going after another longish and troublesome stray hair, "Rimbaud was a flash in the pan." His pronouncement, his "sentencing," was unhesitating and final, and I never asked him anything else. The difference between Levine and Byrd, both at the same college, is like the difference between the music of John Coltrane and Doc Severinsen. One is amazing and a revelation; the other makes you wonder who hired him.

Levine was the funniest and most unflinchingly honest man I have ever known. In those years, class after class would literally shake with laughter. A kind of rare, almost giddy intelligence constantly surfaced in Levine in comments that were so right and so outrageous that they kept us all howling, for he kept brimming over with the kind of insouciant truths most people suppress in themselves, and none of us in the class were spared from those truths about our work, and, by extension, about ourselves. "Amazing! You write like the Duke of Windsor on acid!" he said to one passively stoned, yet remarkably pompous student. Or, to another, "For a moment there your imagination made an appearance in this poem and its loveliness astonished us all, but then . . . right . . . *here*—where you say, 'Love is golden, Daddy, and forever,' the grim voice of Puritan duty comes back in and overwhelms you with a sense of obligation even you couldn't possibly believe in. Remember, in poetry you don't owe anyone a thing." Or: "Look at this absolutely gorgeous line crying out to escape from all its dumb brothers snoring beside it there!" Or, to a young woman who had written a wonderfully sophisticated poem about a detested ski instructor: "'With practiced stance which he has made his own'—notice all of you please, in the deafness of this age, this line. It's amazingly perfect for what it's doing here, lean, scrupulous, and innocent in tone at the outset. And, just now, it's a pentameter that seems to be light-years beyond anything the rest of you can do. Oh, I know you *have* ears, I mean, I can see them right there on the sides of your heads, and yet on some days they strike me as vestigial, like the appendix, and as the age evolves I can see them creeping toward extinction; soon, all that will be left of ears will be their occasional appearance on postage stamps, along with the passenger pigeon, the Great Auk, Adlai Stevenson." Or, to a student full of pretentiously profound yet completely trite statements concerning God, Love, Death, and Time—a two-page endeavor with all the lines italicized in the typescript: "Writing like this suggests that you might need to find something to do with your hands. Tennis is an excellent sport!"

Something animated him. He is the only person I have ever known who seemed to be fully awake to this life, his own and the lives of others. An amazing talker, it surprised me when I noticed how deeply and closely he listened to his students. And when someone was really troubled, a special kind of listening seemed to go on, and there was often a generous if sometimes unsettling frankness in his response.

Why in the world did he care so much about what we did? Because we mattered so much to him, we began to matter to ourselves. And to matter in this way, to feel that what one did and how one wrote actually might make a difference, was a crucial gift Levine gave to each of us. All you had to do was open it, and it became quite clear, after awhile, that only cowardice or self-deceit could keep you from doing that.

His care for us seems all the more amazing when I recall that these years were crucially difficult and ultimately triumphant years for him as a poet. For in 1965 he went to Spain for the first time, and what changed him deeply there is apparent everywhere in the poems of *Not This Pig*. Shortly after this, he would begin to write the poems that constitute the vision of *They Feed They Lion*. What still strikes me as amazing, and right, and sane, was his capacity to share all that energy, that fire, with those around him: students and poets and friends. The only discernible principle I gathered from this kind of generosity seems to be this: to try to conserve one's energy for some later use, to try to teach as if one isn't quite there and has more important things to do, is a way to lose that energy completely, a way, quite simply of betraying oneself. Levine was always totally *there*, in the poems and right there in front of me before the green sea of the blackboard.

It is fashionable now to disparage poetry workshops, and why not? Some of them are so bad that they constitute a form of fraud in which mediocre talents accept tuition from those with no talent whatsoever. After a couple of years, these unemployables graduate, and their teachers, in their aspiring emptiness, get promoted. But to categorically condemn all workshops as a destructive force in our poetry is nonsense, a nonsense best said on a cliff overlooking the ocean at, say, Big Sur, where one can pretend, momentarily, to be Jeffers or some other great

American Original. And much of Jeffers is just awful. How could a man who looked like that in the photos of him on display at Nepenthe write such dull stuff? Was there no one to tell him how bad it was? In contrast, I think of Pound showing Ford Madox Ford some early work, and of Ford laughing so hard upon reading it (they were not humorous poems) that he actually fell onto the floor and rolled around on it squealing with hilarity at the poems. Pound said that Ford's laughter saved him two years of work in the wrong direction. That was a poetry workshop. That laughter, no matter how painful for Pound, was a useful laughter, even a necessary laughter.

Could I have written poems in isolation? I doubt it. I grew up in a town where, in the high school library, Yeats's *Collected Poems* was removed, censored *in fact* because two students had been found laughing out loud at "Leda and the Swan." That left Eliot. For two years, largely in secret, I read and reread Eliot, and I told no one this. But finally one afternoon in journalism class, while the teacher was out of the room, Zamora stretched out, lying over three desk tops, and began yelling at the little, evenly spaced holes in the plyboard ceiling: "O Stars, Oh Stars!" The others around us talked on in a mild roar. Then Zamora turned to me and said: "I saw that book you always got with you. Once again, guy, I see through you like a just-wiped windshield." There was a little pause, and then he said, "What is it, you wanna be a poet?" I said, "Yeah. You think that's really stupid?" His smile had disappeared by the time he answered, "No, it isn't stupid. It isn't stupid at all, but I'd get out of town if I were you."

It was true. A town like that could fill a young man with such rage and boredom that the bars of Saigon might twinkle like a brief paradise. You could die in a town like that without lifting a finger.

Whenever I try to imagine the life I might have had if I hadn't met Levine, if he had never been my teacher, if we had not become friends and exchanged poems and hundreds of letters over the past twenty-five years, I can't imagine it. That is, nothing at all appears when I try to do this. No other life of any kind appears. I cannot see myself walking down one of those streets as a lawyer, or the boss of a packing shed, or even as the farmer my father wished I would become. When I try to do this, no one's there; it seems instead that I simply had never *been* at all. All there is on that street, the leaves on the shade trees that line it curled and black and closeted against noon heat, is a space where I am not.

Strange Days: Zbigniew Herbert
in Los Angeles

The early 1970s. Even now, they still seem to me a strange and extreme time in America. Nixon had just invaded Cambodia, and in Kent, Ohio, on one idyllic spring afternoon, a few nervous National Guardsmen began shooting kids on a college campus. In L.A., late at night on one FM channel, Charlie Manson's "girls," his acolytes, would come on live to tell you to drive immediately to Death Valley to join them because, in the exhausted slang of the times, "it's all . . . you know, coming *down* out there." On the Sunset Strip, the spirit scavengers of all sects were scooping up the penniless and strung-out young as quickly and easily as grunion. And although a large quake brought down some of L.A. and twisted a few freeways into new and inventive shapes, much more remarkable were those homes in the San Fernando Valley that had been simply evacuated afterward—breakfasts congealed on the tables. Those vacant houses . . . what stories they told of the times by saying nothing at all about a past or a future.

What *was* "coming down"? Nixon was, gradually, and in a few years Saigon would fall to those who, evidently, cared most about it. But those events were hidden then. In those first years of the 1970s, each day felt a little like the day after a revolution that had not happened. Phrases like "the summer of love" and "the gathering of the tribes" were used sarcastically. The Haight looked windswept and evacuated when I walked through it one afternoon in 1970.

What *was* "coming down" was Time in the Absolute Present, a Present dressed in so many distracting styles that it was

From *Antioch Review* 45 (winter 1987): 75–83.

possible, in the boundless vanity of the moment, to believe that history was irrelevant. To many people, history meant the literature of failure. Some welcomed its erasure. Some were boasting of having become "postliterate."

During these strange days, I was honored to drive, more or less regularly, the poet Zbigniew Herbert just about anywhere he needed to go. If poets had chauffeurs, I suppose I would have been happy to have been merely his chauffeur. But he never treated anyone like a chauffeur. We quickly became friends. I was young and knew so little that I must have seemed then to possess that innocence peculiar to Americans; in the world it is known simply as ignorance. I was twenty-four and trying to live authentically in the Present. I had no idea that I wasn't, that I was simply living in some benign erasure of the past. But I was lucky. In Zbigniew I had found a friend who was almost a classical isle of sanity.

I remember complaining to him one day as we drove through the suburbs east of downtown L.A. that Whitman now seemed to me a poet exclusively of the nineteenth century. Zbigniew smiled as if the name Whitman carried with it a fragrance of pleasure, like the name of a liberated city. And he kept smiling as he looked directly at me and said: "No, I think he is eternal."

That is the kind of sanity I mean, a radical sanity in which the word *eternal* is made wild once again and authentic. He said it without any trace of condescension or arrogance. Yet the answer was precise and uncompromising.

One doesn't compromise with a word like *eternal*. The term is negotiable only in the mouths of the falsely fashionable *guru* or the well-intentioned revolutionary who doesn't know he is merely the instrument of death. Zbigniew was neither.

At Zip and Go University, where we both taught, Zbigniew was largely unknown. But in Europe he was famous, and even in L.A. he was known in the more worldly circles.

One day, when I picked up Zbigniew to drive him to class, he told me he had gone to a party the night before.

"Where?" I asked.

"In Hollywoooed," he said. That was how he pronounced it: "wooed."

"I didn't know you knew anyone in Hollywood."

"It was Polanski's," he replied matter-of-factly.

"Really? You mean you *know* him? You knew him in Poland?"

"In Warsaw. Yes, since his student days. He asked if I had seen *Rosemary's Baby*. But then he asked me if I liked it. I had to say: 'of *course* not.' He nodded. He still . . . understands. And Roman is a nice boy, good boy."

There was a pause. I wondered if he wished to qualify that last statement, but no, he did not.

"I go make pee-pee, and then we go to the college: yes?"

Ten minutes later we were stuck in traffic on Fair Oaks Boulevard.

The slightly mischievous beaming smile came over his face again. It was the kind of smile that assured anyone in his presence that good fortune was just around the corner for both of you, and that Zbigniew could not imagine being any happier in any other company. It was one quality he had in common with Fitzgerald's Gatsby, and it seemed, in the poet, less a matter of style than of his nature. From the scrupulous, terse classicism of his poems I had imagined the poet must look something like Robinson Jeffers. But Zbigniew was slightly short, slightly plump—and most amazing and disarming of all was his face. His face looked like a sleepy, happy, fledgling bird's face, a wide-face bird—the face of an adolescent barn owl, an owlet.

But Zbigniew walked, often enough, with a limp that plagued him. Sometimes it was more noticeable than it was at other times. I had the distinct suspicion, though I couldn't even now say why, that it had something to do with his participation in the Polish Underground. Sometimes the limp was quite pronounced, as if his leg from the knee down were asleep and would not wake, and then somehow he looked as if he both resented and respected its deep sleep. I never asked him about it.

What T. S. Eliot once said of Blake was true of Zbigniew as far as I knew him: "There was nothing of the superior person about him." Zbigniew was perhaps the most civilized poet I've known. His sense of decency was both unstinting and unshakable.

A student poet, John Bowie, a young man naturally shy around everyone he didn't know well, especially if they were famous, finally got up the nerve to ask Zbigniew if he could show him some of his work. Zbigniew replied, "Only if you will have lunch with me." A look almost approaching awe came over Bowie's face then, a look that suggested, sadly enough, that Bowie had never been treated quite as well by anyone in his entire life. Four years later John Bowie would be dead in Iowa City of a weak heart he never knew he had; and so, looking back upon that little meeting between the two of them, the kindness there, and the pleasure Bowie took from that moment into the rest of his short life, it no longer seems to me that such gestures of open decency and welcome are at all insignificant. If, like John Bowie, you only live to be twenty-five, and if you spend most of that time growing up in a little, bleak, monotonous, stucco suburb like Alhambra, where your father is a television repairman, a lunch like the lunch John Bowie had that day with Zbigniew may be something you take with you all the way to the abrupt, breathless end.

Or think of decency in Nazi-occupied Warsaw: What it means is that you never know if the way you treat a friend today may be the last way you treat him at all.

How different Zbigniew's attitude was from that of a colleague who once said to me, in the corridor where we taught: "Let's use this key and grab the elevator; we'll have to see fewer students that way."

In corridors honeycombed with faculty offices, my colleagues smiled and nodded and said hello repetitively to each other throughout the day. If they stopped smiling and nodding and helloing it usually meant that they planned to kill you. I had to explain this curious custom, which I had just figured out, to Zbigniew, and so I told him when he dropped in after class.

"My face is tired; it has been weight-lifting smiles all day," he said. "My voice also. The Hello Variations. They are extremely difficult, I think, particularly in the *scherzo;* just two notes! Elo? Yellöe. Hélo. And yet, I don't agree. What is more treacherous than one too many smiles?" He paused and looked directly at me for a second. "You don't know, do you? I will tell you then. Five too many smiles; ten too many smiles."

One day Zbigniew and I were driving through Monterey Park, a tedious little town east of L.A., another suburb. Its unvarying barracks of ranch-style townhouses floated by outside. Zbigniew looked out the window at the pale shades of yellow and green and pink, at the nothing that was there. You couldn't see the nothing that was not there, for that was Alhambra, or San Gabriel, or Altadena. But we did pass a park of some kind with a few scrawny trees that looked exhausted and as if they had been recently planted. On the other hand, they looked ancient too, as if they had been trying to grow there, straining at the hard-pan soil under them, since Drake sailed by. Somehow a developer had achieved a look of defeat so permanent that even the future had no future in Monterey Park.

"Sometimes," said Zbigniew, "in communist countries . . . beauty is possible . . . in . . . what do you call it? I forget."

"Architecture?" The word suddenly seemed so grand somehow.

"Yes. Sometimes the state says, O.K. But here is not possible."

"Well, sometimes it is."

"But there is only one solution for L.A."

"A solution? For L.A.? What?"

"Burn it," said Zbigniew, as if the idea was clear to everyone, had been clear for some time now, as if the wholesale torching of everything from Pomona to Hermosa Beach was already on the drawing boards of urban planners. I looked over to see if he was merely kidding, but he kept staring out the window. Perhaps I had not heard him correctly.

Another afternoon, after work. We were waiting for a light to change.

"I cannot drive. If only I could drive a car, then I, even *I*, not a citizen, I could *buy* a car!" The innocent light of that smile came over his face again. So he wanted to buy a car. Well, I thought to myself, wheels can make arson a lot easier.

"You never drove, Zbigniew?"

"Once. I drove once, yes."

"When?"

He was silent for a moment. Then he began. "It was after a meeting of the Underground. The boy who drove for me was waiting in the car. But dead. The Nazis shot him. Just one shot, a style they had. I came out later . . . I saw him. I had to learn fast. I pushed the boy over to other side of car seat. I drove. Just one time. With the dead boy beside me. I drove."

He said all this without any visible emotion. It was stated as fact only. That was his way, or one of his ways. It was all a matter of carving out a style so impermissive of the merely and suspiciously personal, a style so lean and scrupulous and classical, that the poem cast out the poet, and what was said cast out the sayer.

I thought of all the above much later, years later. At the moment of the anecdote, hearing it for the first time, I could think of nothing else but that image. Driving for the first time with a dead boy beside him.

Zbigniew was reading the personal ads in the back of the *L.A. Free Press*. Now and then I would explain the various terms, the abbreviations for gay, black, bisexual, sadomasochism. But some were new to me.

"What does this word mean here, *revolution?* They use it on every page. It means hashish. It means sex. It means sex oils."

It was 1971. They were using it on almost every page, even though it meant nothing now. "Sex oils?" I asked.

"Here," he said, handing me the paper.

"Oh, scented oils. Sure, people use that stuff, some people do."

"Girls in my classes, I think. But where is this *revolution?*"

"They just use it. It sounds exciting, and if you were born yesterday, it sells papers, I guess."

"But hashish, free love, sex oils. That is *fun*. Revolution is not. I was in only one revolution. Against the Nazis. It was necessary. I hated it. I hated them more."

I felt that sudden and peculiar tiredness Americans feel when they have to explain a word their culture has corrupted beyond recognition.

"Zbigniew, over here, in L.A. especially, if the phrase *viva la muerte* made a product sell, like . . . say, soap, for example, they'd use it."

"Really? *Viva la muerte. Long Live Death.* For the name of a soap? Yes, I like it. It's O.K. *Long Live Death* Soap."

Zbigniew had turned on the TV, and now sat before it with the rapt and attentive expression of a child on his face. In Poland, he said, no one owned televisions. I could hear the canned laughter behind a "Lucy" rerun. It sounded like swirling water. Suddenly it felt as if the television had been on all my life.

"Is Ford a good car?" Zbigniew suddenly asked.

"Some of them are," I said.

"Is . . . possible to find, here, *used* Ford?"

Oh, boy.

"Zbigniew, I think you've come to the right place," I said, then watched him turn back to the flickering screen, this man from a country with no televisions and no Fords—where thousands knew his poems by heart.

When Zbigniew's wife, Katrina, arrived from Paris they bought a 1960 light blue four-door Fairlane sedan. Katrina drove it at a more or less unvarying fifty miles per hour through city streets, school zones, alleys, campus parking lots, and posted boulevards throughout the San Gabriel Valley. But on the freeways she held it to an understated seventy-five. Beyond that, I felt, the car would change into something else. Riding with them I'd hold on to the arm rest, and hope. Zbigniew sat in the back seat, answering letters, drawing in his sketchbook. Oblivious, absorbed as a child in what he was sketching, his wide face held something both birdlike and very peaceful within it. He seemed happy with Katrina there, and happy with life. When Katrina had the Ford moving fast enough so that I could hear every hose and gasket singing under the hood and the rods beginning to chatter, she would suddenly turn to us, speaking either Polish or French, since she knew no English. It was as if the road no longer held much interest for her. Above forty-five, the whole car shook, but neither of them seemed to notice.

I remember hearing the utterly incomprehensible Polish rising above the engine noise of that moment. I remember, too, feeling utterly happy.

After a week or so, the Ford went in for repairs. I went to pick them up at the university. Usually they were full of smiles, but today they were silent and preoccupied. I asked Katrina what was wrong.

"De Gaulle est mort," she replied. They rode home in silence, reading about it in the paper. But were they *mourning* de Gaulle? They were, after all, Europeans. They lived *in* history. For Poles of their generation, for a very brief moment, de Gaulle once must have meant a possible future. Their shared memory of this moment might be, someday, all they had left of him after the erasures of history had taken place.

We passed a Shell station, a Taco Bell, a 7–11, Carpet World . . . what was there to remember here? Burn it? Vote with a flame? That was one way, but in Watts, there was at least a history of misery and outrage. But Alhambra? Rosemead? San Gabriel? You can't burn something that isn't there. But of course this is all metaphor. I'd never torch anything larger than a pile of trash.

And yet, I thought, in L.A. or in Warsaw, no one escapes the time into which he is born. It is a particular violation done precisely to him, precisely *now*. In a way we *all* live in history, just as, in another way, we begin to live in a future serenely composed of the erasures of that history.

We passed the small roadhouse near the freeway interchange, the marquee advertising: Live Sex on Stage. For the first time I did not cynically imagine the performers as a tired, strung-out hippy couple going through the motions for car salesmen, small-time executives, bitter housewives, professors who had stopped reading. I imagined that they were both beautiful, that they loved having sex on stage and being watched as they did so, that their orgasms were simultaneous, that their hairstyles were reminiscent of no period of time. Strangely enough, they seemed even less interesting when I thought of them that way.

On their last day in America, Zbigniew and Katrina drove to Yosemite National Park in a rented car. Around one of the curves above the valley's floor they hit a mule deer, a doe. I imagine that it got up just after it was hit, wobbled for a few steps along the roadside, then fell again. I imagine that it kept lifting its head to one side and its still graceful, supple, but slowly benumbed and stiffening neck as it tried to rise again and again—and the blood that had begun to appear a few seconds earlier on its lips now spilled from them, spattering the highway in different random patterns. And because the deer kept swinging its head slowly upward and to one side, I imagine the flecks of blood beginning to appear on its withers, its back, and even on the delicately shocking white of its underbelly. I imagine Zbigniew and Katrina standing there beside it, unable to do anything—until a ranger came and ended it all with one shot from a revolver held to the doe's temple.

They were both, said Phil and Franny Levine later, sick about it. After all, it was their last day in the United States; they had wanted to stay longer, and the death of something that wild must have seemed to hold, for both of them, wider and larger and more mysterious implications.

I don't know because I never heard from either one of them again. We promised to write each other, and one night I sat down and wrote a three-page letter to Zbigniew. Then I tore it up. Perhaps some friendships are meant to exist only in a certain place, at a certain time—three people driving casually around L.A. in a blue Ford. I don't know. I don't know if I was ever meant to know.

Soon after that, I left L.A. I never tried to write to him again.

But my chronicle of these strange days does not end quite yet. I hadn't heard any news of Zbigniew for years, and then, about six years ago, at a party in Berkeley, someone said that Czeslaw Milosz had been in Warsaw and, at a reception for him, Zbigniew came up and asked Milosz if he knew of anyone who could turn down the heat in the room.

"And . . . ?" I asked the man telling the story.

"That's it; that's all I heard," he said, sipping a glass of wine.

"That word *heat*—I wonder if it has some cryptic significance," said a woman standing beside him. Her remark was meant to be adequately clever, and I suppose it was. I had often wondered about Zbigniew, especially with the news of Solidarity. Now I was thinking about him again. I had been afraid the anecdote ended there.

And then, shortly after that, at a reception after he had read in Iowa City, I asked Milosz if he knew how Zbigniew was. Since I was a complete stranger to him, I didn't expect much in the way of a reply, and the party was fairly noisy. I'm not sure he heard me, or, if he had heard me, whether he understood my question. At any rate, he did not answer and a few seconds later someone began speaking to him in Polish.

Even more recently someone wrote me to say that he had heard Zbigniew was in "bad shape," suffering from severe depression and dividing his time between Warsaw and Berlin, where he was in the care of a psychiatrist.

But after all, these are rumors. Poets collect them the way they collect lint, and trouble, and eternity.

After all, the future can't erase everything—can it?

Eden and My Generation

The Connoisseurs of Loss

At least since the Bible and Milton, much of English poetry has been preoccupied with the loss of Eden and the resulting knowledge which partially and paradoxically compensates for all solitary exile. But as myth became, in the artistic *and* general consciousness, more and more possible only in a radically *secular* way, poetry began to locate Eden, not in public myth, but in the privacy of personal experience, and to explore it in the lyric rather than the epic mode. Eden became a real *place;* it could be named, spoken of, lived in, and remembered. The Romantic poets understood Eden, not as an elsewhere, but as a place inside the poet's own life. Wordsworth's landscape becomes, in his recollection, his private, unauthorized, unorthodox Eden. Yet Wordsworth's decision to *make* such a landscape Edenic is a compromise in which he stands, warily but finally, at the center.

In just this fashion, the named, autobiographical, particular *place,* whether Paumanok or Paterson or Big Sur or Vermont, became a way to locate the theme—became, as place, the new and personally experienced Eden. The poetry of my own generation, however, has been turning away or aside from such named, secular but sanctified places. Instead, it generalizes self-consciously about the Edenic theme of loss and exile. And with that change has come a corresponding change in language. This resistance to a resolutely imagistic, autobiographical poetry, and a preference for a more abstract,

This essay was originally delivered as a lecture at the Aspen Writers' Conference in July 1980. Reprinted here from *Field* 26 (spring 1982): 27–46.

meditative mode of thinking testifies not merely to private loss, exile, and knowledge, but to a *collective and generational* loss, exile, and knowledge. The very language used has become increasingly less innocent, or such innocence increasingly less possible. In a way my generation has had to invent a way of thinking and a language which could not only record its losses, but could also question the motive behind every use of that language—especially its own. This need, however, is not only some necessary Oedipal and dialectal agon of one generation reproaching another. It is simply that for my generation there was no access via experience to the Eden of its parents. For to replace Eden in their own expressionist language is simply to mimic Eden or mock it. To find it is to find the words it needs in one's own time.

Place

Donald Hall begins an interesting essay on the nature of place in poetry with the following remarks:

> For some poets, poetry derives from a place. Poem after poem reaches back and touches this place, and rehearses experiences connected with the place: Wordsworth's "Nature"; the Welsh farms of Dylan Thomas; T. S. Eliot's St. Louis and Dry Salvages; Wallace Stevens' Florida; Walt Whitman and Paumanok; architectural Italy for Ezra Pound; Gloucester for Charles Olson . . . But I am not thinking only of poetry which is geographic or descriptive. I am thinking of places which to the poets embody or recall a spiritual state.[1]

But how do poems "embody or recall" these "spiritual" states? Hall's notions here have the flavor of truth, but perhaps it is wisest to realize these ideas specifically, as poems do. To begin with one personal example, the poet Gary Soto's San Joaquin Valley is the same geographical region I am from, and yet his experience of that place, both sacred and blasphemous, is that of a Mexican-American, and it is vastly different from my own experience of it as the son of a farmer, an "Anglo." In a way, we lived side by side, but in different worlds. Similarly, a few miles to the north in Fresno, David St. John was growing up, but in a place which even then considered itself a city. Against that more or less brutal and degenerating ambience, St. John refined his poetry, distilled it, into a bitter elegance. And ninety miles south, in Bakersfield, where *every* variety of vine refuses, finally, to grow, Frank Bidart must have been working. Talking once about his poems, and speaking in defense of their lack of imagery, their brazen love of the abstract statement, I found myself saying that such an aesthetic as his could come only from Bakersfield, that the poems' lack of imagery resembled the impoverishment of their soil. I was naive, of course; it wasn't the poetry of Bakersfield; it was only the poetry of Bidart's *Golden State.* It is the geography of the psyche that matters, not the place.

And so a place in poetry, if it is good poetry, may be a spiritual state and not a geographic one. Compare, for example, T. S. Eliot's Gloucester with Charles Olson's. Similarly, my San Joaquin Valley is like no one else's, even though the same vineyards and towns may appear there. And, obviously, a reader can't learn as much, factually, about a place from a poet as he can from a decent journalist. The place of a *poem*—Levine's Detroit; James Wright's Ohio; Lowell's Boston; the various Northwests of Gary Snyder, Carolyn Kizer, Richard Hugo, William Stafford, David Wagoner; Elizabeth Bishop's Nova Scotia—these are places we can never get to, and not simply because those places, every place, are subject to change and decay, or subject to that peculiarly ominous breeze at the end of Hugo's "Death of Kapowsin Tavern": "wind black enough to blow it all away." Rather, the poet has sealed those places away into the privacies of his or her work forever, so that, as William Gass observed, Joyce's Dublin is vastly superior to the *real* one. In a way, we can never get to those places because they don't exist—not really, anyway. But once, I tried to find such a place. I walked for days through Boston, wondering, idly, how it got there, and why. I did remember one line from Stevens: "The wise man avenges by building his city in snow." But mostly it was the grave, ruefully humorous poetry of Lowell's *Life Studies* that kept ringing quietly in my mind: "Boston's hardly passionate Marlborough Street" (which is actually a phrase Lowell borrows from William James) or "the trees with Latin labels" on Boston

Common (they do have labels!). But then, to mimic Lowell, I was so out of things. At eighteen, I was so Californian I thought even Detroit was an "Eastern" city, and to discover Boston through Lowell was like trying to discover Italy through Ezra Pound. I felt like a tourist with one of the most idiosyncratic and beautiful guidebooks ever written. But I did feel like a tourist. *Life Studies* gave me a way to *feel* a place which was not there anymore. It could never be there at all for me, really, for Lowell's Boston childhood and harrowing adult life consists primarily of what Bachelard would call "intimate" space—Lowell's poems usually occur in closed rooms, in privacies ("endurable and perfect") given up to him by his memory. It is not surprising that Lowell traces the inception of the first poem he wrote for *Life Studies* to the obsessive, recurring image of a "blue, china door-knob." And no doubt, by the time I arrived, someone else was living at 91 Revere Street. I don't know; I was too shy to go up and knock.

Place in poetry, then, or for that matter in much fiction, is often spiritual, and yet it is important to note that this spiritual location clarifies itself and becomes valuable only through one's absence from it. Eden becomes truly valuable only after a fall, after an exile that changes it, irrecoverably, from what it once was. When I returned to California in 1970 to teach, I returned to a withered Eden, and there was, all around me, even in the cool cynicism of stoned kids on Hollywood Boulevard, enough to confirm its demise. In one of his earlier poems, Robert Hass phrased that demise in strict couplets: "My God it is a test, / This riding out the dying of the West." Fallen, I returned to my home, and, if I did not have any real vision then, I did have eyesight. I could see the place—that is one of the consequences of falling.

It is no wonder, then, that Donald Hall, in his essay, goes on to ask:

> What kind of place must it be? It must be a place where we felt free. It must be a place associated not with school or with conventional endeavor or with competition or with busyness. It must be a place, therefore, in which we can rehearse feelings (and a type of thinking) which belong in evolutionary terms to

an earlier condition of humanity. And it is this earlier mind that we wish to stimulate, in poetry. Sometimes we speak as if we wish to return to it; actually, we want it to return to us, and to live with us forever. Therefore the place which is golden is a place where we have loafed and invited the soul, and where the ego—not yet born—has made no demands on the soul.[2]

Perhaps all of this *is* true, even the earlier mind theory, if only in the substrata of the poet's memory. And yet the particular struggle, the agon and play which is a poem, usually records, laments, or testifies to our distance from this "golden place." That may be why, when Robert Hass writes a later and more analytical poem, "Meditation at Lagunitas," he begins by saying: "All the new thinking is about loss. / In this it resembles all the old thinking." It is almost as if, from "Tintern Abbey" to Lowell's "Grandparents," variations on the same theme were struck up, in different chords. Even if we look at one of the most Edenic and pastoral of modern poems, Dylan Thomas's "Fern Hill," the poet's final agony is apparent when he concludes: "And wake to the farm forever fled from the childless land. / Oh as I was young and easy in the mercy of his means, / Time held me green and dying / Though I sang in my chains like the sea." It is only in his absence from such a farm that he can see its paradoxical meaning, that one is always in a state of becoming, and that one is always, also, becoming nothing. If we endure our Edens, Thomas says, and that is what we must do, all easy jubilation ends.

But suppose a poet does not leave his home, his place, does not fall from his Eden, but in fact seems to stay there, as James Wright seems to stay, through memory and imagination, in his native Ohio? But how can any Eden endure the Self? Much of the painful power and beauty in Wright's work comes from his witnessing the decay of his place:

> For a proud man,
> Lost between the turnpike near Cleveland
> And the chiropractors' signs looming among dead mulberry
>   trees,
> There is no place left to go
> But home.

He has almost said, or he may as well have said: "There is no home left to go to." When we fall, we begin to know, we begin to see. To stay in that special, spiritual place is, simply, to watch its dismemberment through time. As we mature, or just grow older, we are given *sight,* or rather our memories give us a particularly subjective (hence objective and objectifying) ability to remember what once was in distinction to what is, at each moment, around us. Such imagery, such memory and witnessing, affords the Ohio of James Wright much of its power. Even the place-names, "Wheeling Steel," "Benwood," "Marion," participate in a past, not a present. The same is true of Lowell's *Life Studies,* Levine's *1933,* Gerald Stern's *Lucky Life,* Snyder's *Myths & Texts,* Bishop's *Geography III,* Robert Penn Warren's *Or Else*—the possible list is endless. Even if a poet chooses not to name his place, as Stanley Kunitz chooses in his poem, "Father and Son," the remembered place, the pond, becomes a radiance.

For many, of course, my idea of the Edenic will seem difficult to accept, or it will appear archaic, or merely silly. As a concept, it aligns itself so clearly to the Bible and to Milton that it seems permanently to recall its sources, and to recall orthodox conceptions of sin, guilt, death, sex, or at least the knowledge of these. But I intend the term only in its loosest, and perhaps most relevant, sense: that is, I may not believe in the myth of the Fall, but it is still possible for me to feel *fallen.* Why? Because I can see, and perhaps because the myth and the feeling is explainable as Freud explains it, in *Civilization and Its Discontents:*

> Originally the ego includes everything, later it detaches itself from the outside world. The ego-feeling we are aware of now is thus only a shrunken vestige of a more extensive feeling—a feeling which embraced the universe and expressed an inseparable connection of the ego with the external world. If we may suppose that this primary ego-feeling has been preserved in the minds of many people—to a greater or lesser extent—it would co-exist like a sort of counterpart with the narrower and more sharply outlined ego-feeling of maturity, and the ideational content belonging to it would be precisely the notion of limitless extension and oneness with the universe—the same feeling as that described by my friend as "oceanic."[3]

Later elaborations of this, perhaps even Lacan's "stade du miroir" theory, attest to similar separations. In his essay on the growth of landscape painting, Rilke phrases the idea with a simpler grandeur: "For men only began to understand Nature when they no longer understood it; when they felt that it was the Other, indifferent towards men, without senses by which to apprehend us, then for the first time they stepped outside of Nature, alone, out of a lonely world."

Poetry, the poetry of the spiritual place, can remind us, then, of the Edenic, even of the "oceanic." What seems to be a curious phenomenon of nineteenth- and twentieth-century poetry in particular is that the Edenic or "oceanic" is often retrievable only through a poem with a highly *specified* place: "Tintern Abbey"; "Little Gidding"; "Brooklyn Bridge"; "Patterson"; "Paumanok"; "Gloucester"; "Dover Beach"; the New Englands of Dickinson and Frost; the South of Dickey, Penn Warren, Tate, Jarrell, Ransom; Jeffers's Big Sur; Bly's Minnesota. This involvement with place, from Romantic and modernist poets to the present, has come about in part I think because a poet wants to locate himself or herself somewhere, to be "a man (or woman) speaking to men (or women)"; it is also a way of testifying to the demand and limitations of lyrical experience, to say: "I was the man, I suffered, I was there." The lyric wishes to be antidogmatic, nondidactic, *honest*. Williams articulated the idea this way: "It is in the wide range of the local only that the general can be trusted for its one unique quality, its universality." And "the local" is that vestige of the "oceanic" which Freud says we carry within ourselves, withered, out of childhood. And it is *there,* in the place recalled by the poet, the sacred home. It can't be otherwise, the poems seem to tell us—the holy place is a few miles above Tintern Abbey; or is just under a particular cedar growing in the place of a vanished New England farm town in Frost's "Directive"; or it is in the burned-out remains of Hugo's Kapowsin Tavern; or in Levine's unburned Detroit in 1952; or on a mountaintop in the Cascades where Gary Snyder pauses, "between heaven and earth," before going down "to stand in lines in Seattle, looking for work." It will be there, or nowhere, the poems *deceive us* into believing. Actually, reading such poems, we discover, excavated by another's feeling, those places in ourselves.

However, I don't intend to suggest that poets write only about such places. They don't. And there are any number of strong poets whom I cannot associate with any particularized place, such as Creeley, Strand, Ashbery, Rich, and Merwin. And yet because of the predominance of place, especially in American poetry of recent decades, it is only to be expected that a turning away from a particular, named, autobiographical poetry of place might occur, and this is what I believe is happening in the work of some of the younger poets writing now. I should say that this poetry, abstract or meditative as it might be, is not new, however—see Rilke and Stevens. And I also want to say that even when this poetry is at its most meditative, the inhabiting or recalling of a spiritual place continues, and without serious impediments. But first I think it is important to speculate, at least for my own purposes here, on what sort of shift has occurred, and to ask why it has occurred. For to turn away from one's own autobiographical, personal memory of a particular place is to appear, often enough, to have accomplished a dismissal of one tradition: that of the alienated, isolated artist.

And yet most younger poets still testify precisely to this alienation and isolation, this falling from Eden. Only they have changed it. It is as if the whole tradition has become, by now, shared, held in common, a *given*—or as if the poems confer the same sort of loss upon all of us, not only upon the privately suffering poet. And yet for a while, in the late sixties and early seventies in this country, it seemed to me that almost every American poem was going to locate itself within a more or less definite place, was going to be spoken usually in the first-person singular, and would involve, often, the same kind of testimony to the poet's isolation. The problem of that poetic stance was, unfortunately, its real power—its irresistibly attractive, usually imagistic surface. So many young poets, responding honestly to the work of Bly, Wright, Snyder, Plath, Stafford, or Merwin, tended to write poems that looked stylistically imitative, even derivative, of those and of other poets. That imitative gesture began to feel faint, inauthentic, often simply insincere or naive. And finally, as if in despair of recreating the reality of prior visions, this poetry often took on a sarcastic or sardonic attitude toward experience (some of the

dark humor of James Tate and Bill Knott might be read as a
visionary reaction to older poets) and toward place itself, as in
Cynthia MacDonald's funny satire of Bly's Midwest, in which
an otherwise sensible young woman gives up her prior life,
and, following Bly's advice, moves to South Dakota and
spends the rest of her years working in a service station, far
from anything except a randomly passing client. But many of
the poems were not informed by any satirical purpose. They
were *serious* and heartfelt. Even so, too many of the poems
about Ohio or Illinois really began to merely anthologize a
few clichés or commonplaces about the Midwest—clichés
available to anyone who can read the cartoons in the *New
Yorker,* or worse luck, the *Reader's Digest.* Often, the cartoons
in the *New Yorker* at least were much more imaginative than
some of the poems. The vast increase in small magazines, in
the sheer number of them, seems in retrospect to have had
nothing to do with authenticating American places: often the
poets had no interest in becoming the mythographers of the
place in which they happened to be anyway, and so Gary
Snyder's advice to this effect had little sway. What did this
kind of poem typically look like? I will quote only one ex-
ample, a poem called "Driving East"—I am withholding the
name of the poet, however, because this is, for him, a very
early poem, and because his later and more mature work
seems to me very beautiful and haunting:

> For miles,
> the snow is on all sides of me,
> waiting.
> I feel like
> a lot of empty cattle yards,
> my hinges swing open to the wind.

Pretty, yes, but as a whole it is just too easy. Besides, hinges
don't swing open to the wind; gates do. Too often the poet
could look like a tourist dressed in some other poet's style, and
style itself, as is usually the case in America, became too impor-
tant. More seriously, place meant nothing very important to
these poets, and nothing very spiritual, and such a poetry
wasn't even "regional." The larger problem, obvious by now,

was that there simply wasn't much experience or craft in poems such as "Toledo, Ohio, as Seen from the Balcony of the Holiday Inn." What had been a truly visionary prospect in the poetry of James Wright or Philip Levine became trivialized in the more immature imitations. But I am not maligning anyone, here, for being influenced. There probably isn't any other way to learn how to write poetry.

Still, so many of the poets of the sixties and seventies had no place to go—and no home worth returning to.

Again, in some unspecifiably social sense, it may be that places themselves became, throughout much of America, so homogenized that they became less and less available as spiritual locations, shabbier and sadder. A friend from Alabama once lamented to me that he had, as a young fiction writer, no South left to write about, that the topless bars and McDonald's in Birmingham were like topless bars and McDonald's everywhere. He could only imagine a South that had disappeared, and this was a literary South. But to create such an imagined place in spite of the reality around him would eventually make him participate in a merely literary regionalism. And the problem with a poem, or a story, that is strictly regional is its vulnerability (like those too numerous photographs of collapsed barns) to time. For example, it is still possible for me to admire Sandburg's "Chicago," but much of my admiration for it must be mixed with indistinct feelings of nostalgia, distrust, even embarrassment. Yes, I say, Chicago is strong, and its ugliness is a variety of the Beautiful, and yet it is impossible not to know that what Sandburg celebrates is as corny as it is destructive. The poem has matured into a period piece. With shrewder art, this is not the case. For example, old brick buildings in New York can seem charming to me, even powerfully evocative, but then I remember that they are so evocative in this very precise way because I am remembering Edward Hopper's *Early Sunday Morning*, which is not, by the way, regional at all, but great. In a way, I don't, or can't, because of Hopper, see the place at all. Thus, sometimes, the world can turn comically into, and mimic, the art we thought was *about* it. But where the title of *regionalist* is conferred, isn't there a sense, too, of the anachronistic about the region, if not the artist? The regional dissolves almost too obediently into the picturesque. So *Spoon*

River Anthology, in which Masters is often brilliant, remains *regional*. It survives, but it survives, like any truly regionalist poem, like those curious museum towns in New England, like the Maine town in "Skunk Hour" which Lowell satirizes— what once was vital and real comes down to a matter of a few old buildings, kept chronically on display, and housing a boutique, a restaurant, or antique shops. In a way, the *patina* used by the regionalist resembles the renovations of the decorator: it obscures the place. And yet, I am not advising anyone to move into the extreme alternative; besides, no one, knowing what he or she cannot possibly not know about American cities today, could justifiably celebrate Chicago as Sandburg once could celebrate it. But then, poets don't necessarily celebrate Chicago or Denver or Los Angeles, they celebrate loss, they celebrate Eden—the myth of the place in the psyche.

Now it would be easy, and too convenient, to divide older and younger poets into two groups: older poets who appear to have places, and homes, and younger poets who are writing a more abstract, contemplative, unlocalized poetry. Any distinction along these lines would be sophomoric and wrong, however. There are many younger poets who identify themselves with one or more places, and who do this, who claim a place, in methods that renew the tradition of older poets. Robert Hass, Dave Smith, Carolyn Forché, Greg Pape, David St. John, and Stanley Plumly are all poets whose work displays a strong attachment to place. Yet they are never limited *by* place, and often write a poem which could happen anywhere.

And yet, so many younger poets today seem to have no home worth returning to, or worth specifying in the way that Hass specifies the Bay Area of California, or Gary Soto specifies the San Joaquin Valley, or Smith specifies his particular region of the South. Jon Anderson, Thomas Lux, Laura Jensen, Michael Ryan, Tess Gallagher, Daniel Halpern, Marcia Southwick, and so many others appear to have experienced a kind of orphaning by and in America. It may be that this experience, this new homelessness, is what a number of these new poets have in common when they practice the "meditational" mode—for what they tend to hold in common is, at heart, a contradiction: an intimate, *shared* isolation. This isolation is a growth of all the older isolations, but the nature of it has been somewhat changed. Instead of the private loneliness of the first-person point of view, there appears to be, even when unstated, a narrator who behaves as a "we" rather than an "I." Another distinction in this work is its reliance upon increasingly abstract statement and metaphors rather than upon image only. It is interesting to witness Robert Hass, a poet of place if there ever was one, in a sort of transition from one method to another. (I should note here, that many other poets are involved in the same kind of shift, and that it is dramatically obvious in David St. John's *Hush* and *The Shore*.) For what occurs in Hass's poem, "Meditation at Lagunitas," is memory, autobiography—but also the turning away of the poet from the place he confronts and from the poet he once was. It is as if the reader bears witness to a poet seeing through his own need for a place, for location. Truth is not at Lagunitas; it is within the meditation itself. And though this was always the case, Hass stresses it through the larger, abstract claims he makes in the poem.

Meditation at Lagunitas

All the new thinking is about loss.
In this it resembles all the old thinking.
The idea, for example, that each particular erases
the luminous clarity of a general idea. That the clown-
faced woodpecker probing the dead sculpted trunk
of that black birch is, by his presence,
some tragic falling off from a first world
of undivided light. Or the other notion that,
because there is in this world no one thing
to which the bramble of *blackberry* corresponds,
a word is elegy to what it signifies.
We talked about it late last night and in the voice
of my friend, there was a thin wire of grief, a tone
almost querulous. After a while I understood that,
talking this way, everything dissolves: *justice,
pine, hair, woman, you and I.* There was a woman
I made love to and I remembered how, holding
her small shoulders in my hands sometimes,
I felt a violent wonder at her presence
like a thirst for salt, for my childhood river
with its island willows, silly music from the pleasure boat,

muddy places where we caught the little orange-silver fish
called *pumpkinseed*. It hardly had to do with her.
Longing, we say, because desire is full
of endless distances. I must have been the same to her.
But I remember so much, the way her hands dismantled
    bread,
the thing her father said that hurt her, what
she dreamed. There are moments when the body is as
    numinous
as words, days that are the good flesh continuing.
Such tenderness, those afternoons and evenings,
saying *blackberry, blackberry, blackberry.*

The focus of the poem throughout is either directly or tangen-
tially upon the problem of language itself—its uses, its illu-
sions. In this sense the poem's vision is only partly personal,
for Hass's speculations come as much from philosophical con-
siderations, from Lacan or Derrida, as from his own experi-
ence. In fact, I think Hass would stress, *does* stress in the poem,
that thinking itself amounts to experience, to a life, just as any
other thing we do—play, work, sex, talking—amounts to a
life.

As *art* the poem is considerably calmer, seemingly more
detached and reasonable in its phrasings than much of the
poetry which flourished in the late sixties or early seventies.
There is nothing very surreal in Hass's methods, no concern
over a deepening image, and in the poem's imagistic modesty
there may be even a buried admonition (if only to the poet
himself) that the impulse and gesture which can willfully cre-
ate a wild imagery for its own sake is perhaps not worth the
trouble, is perhaps even aesthetically disingenuous or dishon-
est. The grain of such a calm is real: the poet is free of what
Stevens called "the pressure of reality," and he is at least al-
lowed a place for meditation. The poem resists mere auto-
biography through a rapt, abstract energy or impulse. Hass
has no sooner introduced the woman into his poem than she
is, at least until his conclusion, dismissed. For a moment she
even turns into a *law:* "Longing, we say, because desire is full /
of endless distances. I must have been the same to her." But
Hass is so conscious of what he is doing! He is conscious
enough, even, to distrust the very method of thinking which

has afforded his poem, and so, at poem's end, he returns to the truth of remembered, personal experience; then characteristically, revealingly, he generalizes such experience: "Such tenderness, those afternoons and evenings, / saying *blackberry, blackberry, blackberry.*"

And yet how traditional Hass's poem is in its use of a spiritual place! Hass's river, the river of his childhood, provides the same Eden any other poem might. It is much more modest, of course, than Wordsworth's Wye, and it appears, as Hass mentions it, so casually, even minimal, a random memory, though it is not. What is a little surprising, however, is the way in which Hass suppresses the name of that river, Feather or Sacramento, from his poem. Why? It is obvious that the name of the river does not figure importantly in his purposes here, and yet the fact that it does not is, to my way of thinking, full of implications. To name a place, in memory, is to singularize the Self, to individuate the Self, and to maintain belief in the power of the place *through* its name. But the intimation of this poem as a whole suggests that the New Intimacy of Hass or of other poets now working has gone or is going beyond the need for specified locations, and that naming itself, as a first human and poetic act, is what Hass is analyzing here into a sensuous mystery. For the entire, final burden of the poem depends on its success in reminding us that speech is pleasure, and that, paradoxically, the repetition of a word actually empties that word of meaning, of association—which is Hass's earlier fear in the poem. A place, any place, therefore, could be said only to exist *after* language itself, and to be subsequent to language, or created by it. Hass's poem intends, like so many poems since the Romantics, to create the same spiritual place, but Hass is more aware of his traditions, of exactly what he is doing, and it is this which allows him to suggest that we are baptized, not into a location, not into any body of water, but into names, into a river of names. "A word is elegy to what it signifies" because the word is a reality as much as its referent. The new thinking about loss resembles the old thinking about loss exactly through the use of language, through poetry. The more we try to return to the Edenic place, the more our methods, our words, lock us out and turn the pain of our collective separation and exile into poetry. This is not exactly a victory, the poem reminds us, because you can't make love to a poem, and, in "Meditation at Lagunitas," it is sex that recalls Eden more honestly, more innocently and inarticulately, than art does.

And ultimately, a conscious attending to a collective loss is a little different from an attention to a private or confessional loss, even though the same sympathies may occur, finally, as a product of the poem. This poetry, as Stanley Plumly so rightly observed, is often haunted by an Idea more than an Image, a Mind more than a Life. There is a steadiness of control about it, and a poet like Jon Anderson is fond of collapsing private griefs and the singularity and isolation of the poet by stressing, in his own rather austere loneliness and alienation ("My grief is that I bear no grief / And so I bear myself"), how deeply such loss is intimately shared by others: "My friends and I have all come to the same things." In another poem, while passing houses at night, he says: "Each had a father. / He was telling a story so hopeless, / So starless, we all belonged." Below the "I" in Anderson's work there is often the abstract argument of a "we"—friends and loved ones. This "we" never lets us forget our participation in the poem, our inclusion by *it*.[4]

These distinctions can be clarified or thrown into higher relief more or less simply, I think. When Robert Lowell writes, in "Memories of West Street and Lepke,"

> Only teaching on Tuesdays, book-worming
> in pajamas fresh from the washer each morning,
> I hog a whole house on Boston's
> "hardly passionate Marlborough Street,"

he is intimating, through the naming of a place, a private, autobiographical experience. Its virtues are very much like those of realism in fiction. He is saying, like Huck Finn, *this is what happened to me*. His narration will be, therefore, modest, insular, unpretentious, without a sermon for the reader. The reader can respond to the honesty or sincerity of that first-person pronoun, that "I." If a poet says, on the other hand, "Much that is beautiful must be discarded / So that we may resemble / A taller impression of ourselves," our whole experience of the poem will be dramatically different, and we will be much more aware that the poet (John Ashbery), in his choice of method, is both criticizing the alternative and more personal mode at the same time he is admonishing his audience, through his collaborative theme, against the choice, suicide, which the character in his poem has made. In a larger, historical sense, I am aware that both of these methods, in varying degrees of popularity and use, have always been at large in poetry. And of course as *methods* both are very much in use now, and neither one is superior, as an aesthetic choice, to the other. But they are different. Why have so many younger poets now working adopted the latter, the second method? It is often suggested that the influence of Ashbery has had something central to do with this, but I have my doubts that this is entirely true. I think that all of us, finally, live and have to live within a much larger and more various culture than the culture of poetry, and it is impossible for me to forget that most younger poets came of age in the late sixties and early seventies, a time of real trouble in America. What I most remember, and what seems to me most valuable, even though it is now a subject of easy satire, is the sense of shared convictions and tenderness among my generation at that time. There was, for a while, a feeling of community, however frail or perishable, which mattered, and which is not apparent in the chic, lame, New Left political rhetoric of the time—a frustrated rhetoric. So often what one felt as shared or communal could not quite be spoken or brought into speech, much less into poetry. Poets of an older generation, responding to that era and those pressures, wrote mostly out of singular agonies. If they were excessive at times in their use and dependence upon hyperbole and imagery, I think that the sheer ugliness of U.S. foreign policy might have had as much to do with that as the influence of Latin American translations. Often the insistence, in their work, on the beauty of the wild or surreal was a reflex of their anger. In retrospect, I think that what the poets of my generation experienced was not only a deep suspicion of any easy political rhetoric, but a suspicion of what began to seem to be poetical rhetoric as well, of a mannered imagistic poem which effectively kept the poet away from his or her experience. And if that generation felt an enormous disillusionment with the society itself, it felt, also and finally, an equally real disappointment with itself and with its inability to do the impossible task which it had promised itself to do, to reconstruct an Edenic place out of America. I have a clear memory of walking on a cold, winter day through the Haight-Ashbury district in 1970—a place that looked as if it was being evacuated before an approaching army. But there was no army coming. No one, anymore, was coming. There were only young men in pairs who would pass by on each side of me, asking if I wanted to buy acid or speed. The place looked, as someone said, like "a teen-age slum." And the subsequent phenomenon of hip boutiques in suburban shopping centers was not a solution to any problem; it was merely a betrayal of values, and a continuance (how could it be otherwise?) of capitalist culture. When Vietnam ended, my generation appeared, oddly enough, to be so much a part of the culture it had resisted. It was like America, or it was America. Without an enemy, it could not continue.

If the "we" of the younger poets is a plural pronoun, it is also obsessed with loss, but I think it is a loss more profound than the loss of political goals or partisan feelings. Part of what got lost is the possibility of wholly believing in the grand fiction of Romantic alienation and individuation. And yet the new poetry, the "meditative" poetry, appears to be an outgrowth of the more isolated imagistic thinking, and its subject, like that of its parents, is precisely that same testimony to alienation and loss. But it is a collective loss more than a private one. It would be comforting to think that even *collective,* as used here, might have some vestigial political significance, but the loss usually attested to has little to do with political solutions. In fact, the poems seem intensely wary of any political diction, seem to avoid it with great skill, for to locate one's loss in political terms is to locate it within time. But the loss and fall from the Edenic place is final, mythic, a thing that cannot be changed. To talk of it, to talk of some collective loss, means, quite possibly, to deflect one's attention from the subject which provokes the poem. In Marvin Bell's poem "Stars Which See, Stars Which Do Not See" the *ut pictura poesis* of *La Grande Jatte* is both oblique and searingly personal.

They sat by the water. The fine women
had large breasts, tightly checked.
At each point, at every moment,
they seemed happy by the water.
The women wore hats like umbrellas
or carried umbrellas shaped like hats.
The men wore no hats and the water,
which wore no hats, had that well-known
mirror finish which tempts sailors.
Although the men and women seemed at rest
they were looking toward the river
and some way out into it but not beyond.
The scene was one of hearts and flowers
though this may be unfair. Nevertheless,
it was probable that the Seine had hurt them,
that they were "taken back" by its beauty
to where a slight breeze broke the mirror
and then its promise, but never the water.

Deflection? The name of a river. What matters is that the
poem withholds its private sufferer, its poet, so that the place
can be seen, and the common misery of the inhabitants can
be seen: "it was probable that the Seine had hurt them,"
because the place is the location of their loss. The figures
in the painting, the withheld figures they stand for, cannot
quite understand the nature of their loss, and so blame it on
the Seine, deflect what they can no longer articulate onto the
river, the place itself, which changes and does not change,
but does not undergo the final change of the observers, those
whose promise is broken by nothing outside themselves as
they are reminded of it by something as ordinary as a "slight
breeze."

What is it, then, that one loses? That everyone loses? Where
I grew up, the specific place meant everything. As a child in
California, I still thought of myself, almost, as living in the
Bear Flag Republic, not in the United States. When I woke,
the Sierras, I knew, were on my right; the Pacific was a two-
hour drive to my left, and everything between belonged to
me, *was* me. I was astonishingly sheltered. It was only gradu-
ally that I learned the *ways* in which place meant everything,
learned that it meant two hundred acres of aging peach trees

which we had to prop up, every summer, with sticks to keep the limbs from cracking under the weight of slowly ripening fruit. It meant a three-room schoolhouse with thirty students, and meant, also, the pig-headed, oppressive Catholic Church which, as far as I could determine, wanted me to feel guilty for having been born at all. And it meant the gradual self-effacement and aging of my parents. Even in high school when I began to write, even when I hated the place most, and when I rejoiced when I read that Rimbaud (at fourteen!) called his hometown of Charlesville a "shit-hole"—even when the desire to get away was strongest, I was dimly aware that my adolescent hatred of the place was transforming it, was slowly nurturing an Eden from which I was already exiling myself. After I had left for good, all I really needed to do was to describe the place exactly as it had been. That I could not do, for that was impossible. And that is where poetry might begin.

NOTES

1. Donald Hall, "The Poet's Place," in *Goatfoot Milktongue Twinbird* (Ann Arbor: University of Michigan Press, 1978), 205–7.

2. Hall, "The Poet's Place," 207.

3. Sigmund Freud, *Civilization and Its Discontents* (New York: W. W. Norton, 1962), 15.

4. I notice that Ira Sadoff, in his article on meditative poetry (*American Poetry Review*, September–October 1980) uses the same examples of Hass and Anderson for his argument. I think it is curiously substantiating that both of us, two poets working unbeknownst to each other, should come up with the same examples.

Oaxaca and the Politics of Looking

In the late 1960s and early 1970s, Oaxaca was a kind of hippie watering hole. Kids flocked to it because it was so inexpensive (it still is) and because it was therefore possible to "hang out" for an extended stay, one often prolonged by the then abundant supply of mushrooms and fairly decent marijuana. Except for a few strays most have gone now—south to San Cristóbal or west to Puerto Escondido and the beaches. At a certain point the Oaxacan authorities, a friend told me, simply got tired of them and rounded them up and sent them home. Or sent them to jail until they could remember where they did, in fact, *live*. Oaxaca may be poor but it is civilized, and perhaps the police simply became annoyed at having to rouse, each night, stoned blonde teenagers asleep under the hedges of the plaza. Perhaps they drove them out because they bought so little—not even chicklets or gardenias from the street children selling them in the cafés. Anyway, they aren't there now, and not that many casual tourists get this far south. Oaxaca still isn't fashionable. A friend who lives in San Miguel de Allende once told me: "Don't go to Oaxaca. It's got nothing but beggars and disease."

Most of the travelers who come to Oaxaca now come to visit the ruins at Monte Alban or Mitla, cities of the vanished. The pyramids rise like puzzles beneath the clear sky of the mountains. About them there is a sense of almost military order and no suggestion of the usual alterations caused by the encroachments of other ideas and subsequent inhabitants. Monte Alban looks as if it had been simply evacuated overnight. One has the feeling that the stones there dream of no one (if stones could dream), perhaps because—except for a few now anonymous

From *Close Up*, published by Polaroid (winter 1986): 2–10.

priests and rulers, and in accordance with ancient Zapotec belief—no one person finally mattered all that much. By the time the Zapotecs had moved on and built Mitla, a few miles to the south, they had even stopped representing their gods as animals. At Mitla God was abstract—a design repeated endlessly in every wall of the city, a design with about a thousand variations, all of them slight. To see either place is to see something finished, closed off to any future, and certainly closed off to any observer. Whatever their secret was, they took it with them, and those who were left converted quietly over the centuries to Catholicism.

In the parking lot and out of sight of the low hills surrounding Monte Alban, a number of campesinos sell their wares, statues, and figurines. It is entirely possible, I am told, that if one takes enough care he can purchase some authentic bit of art from one of the tombs there. It is possible; it is also against the law. But no one needs to worry all that much. It is much more likely that he will purchase some well-made copy of an actual relic—something in jade even, and modeled after a piece in the famous Tamayo collection in downtown Oaxaca—worth every peso he paid for it.

But for me, the ruins are not the real mystery of Oaxaca; the plaza is. Even now, when I think of it, it seems to rush too willingly into my memory and to blossom there as a kind of permanent pleasure. I lived a block away from it on the Avenida Trujano, a street of low, impoverished, pastel buildings that seemed, except for the linear imposition of the avenue itself, to be caught in a state of inconsequential anarchy against the city's blueprint. But the street, nevertheless, led to the plaza. I always felt better on the plaza; everyone always felt better on the plaza—better, in fact, than most people have the right to feel.

It is difficult to explain this pleasure, for the plaza in Oaxaca is simply a working plaza. Certainly it has almost nothing in common with the huge, barren *zócalo* in Mexico City, with its handful of chronic demonstrators and its long, empty, windswept afternoons in which your heels echo when you cross it. But Oaxaca's *zócalo* differs from more famous plazas as well. In Rome I visited the Piazza Navona to meet friends there but also because it is a sort of obligatory pilgrimage to a grand but by now untouchable past. Even though our century is proud of all it knows about that past, such knowledge begins to seem brittle, as if time itself, benign but inexorable, had made the Piazza Navona more inscrutable, not less so. The Bernini fountain, when I look at it, seems too much like the ruins at Monte Alban or Mitla. It insists on proclaiming its separation and distance from all that I am, insists on intimating that *I* have lost touch with *it*—or that we, as a culture, have done so, and that it neither belongs nor wishes to belong to us.

Perhaps this is inevitable. One of my old teachers once suggested that the time in which anyone is born is a particular violation done to him, and one from which he can never recover. And I agree. But what I like about the plaza in Oaxaca is the fact that it is alive, and has no real subservience to a past. The architectural proportions of it are, as the guidebook will tell you, more Gallic and neoclassical than Spanish colonial. At any rate, no one feels dwarfed by monuments to the dead there, for there is a distinct and pleasant absence of the obligatory statues to heroes that plague most parks. The only memorial, if you could in fact call it that, is amusing. Above the bandstand each night, summer and winter, they turn on the Christmas lights. The kind of lights you can purchase in any drugstore, they don't commemorate Christ as much as the nightly happiness of music in the plaza.

Oaxaca has a history. It is there, in the preserved walls of the regional museum or in the Ruffino Tamayo Museum— his home now a showcase for pre-Columbian artifacts. It is there in the preserved home of Benito Juarez and, two blocks away, in the Cathedral of Santo Domingo, which is a kind of shrine in Mexico. And yet the inhabitants of Oaxaca seem oblivious to this past, or blessedly unaware of it. For cities that are conscious of their past are necessarily self-conscious; they must endure the indignity of restoration and the patina of the renovator until they appear to us as museums, are in fact offered to us as such. Beneath all the plaques in Vienna commemorating Freud or Kafka or Alban Berg there is another more invisible kind of activity that goes on; it is the past encroaching upon the present until the present surrenders itself to it.

By contrast Oaxaca seems innocent, alive. The plaza is

something that has been soiled and consecrated by human use, human necessity, and mistake. Each day it fills with street vendors and with Indians selling baskets and woven goods and little squawking toys and stones carved into small animals. It fills with shoeshine boys and girls selling gardenias from baskets they carry on their heads. It fills with *Oaxaqueño* businessmen and secretaries and ordinary workers and campesinos in from the fields. It is a market; it is a world. None of this is extraordinary if you are Mexican and live in Oaxaca. But if you are simply a traveler or a tourist or someone addicted to ruins and the study of ruins, or if you are, like me, a kind of "*zócalo* rat," then there's only one thing to do: look.

For looking, simply gazing, is one of the great human pleasures; it is also one of the cheapest. And it becomes increasingly important because there are places now that cannot be looked at all. I think of the sickening florescence of shopping malls that use the idea of a plaza but mock it with their ineradicably commercial appetites. Behind them, the barracks of suburban housing stretch for miles. These are places where the eye can starve. But it cannot starve in Oaxaca.

The most obvious and also most banal observation anyone could make about the plaza in Oaxaca is that it is "colorful." It is more difficult to resuscitate that cliché of tour guides than to say *how* it is colorful. For color itself has a good deal to do with the secret of Oaxaca. And that secret has something even greater to do with childhood. It seems that colors were brighter, deeper, more various in hue and shading when I was a child, and this is the way they still are in Oaxaca. It is as if color itself, along with the city, has not quite grown up; certainly it has not grown old. In fact, it seems as if colors have remained in an earlier phase of childhood, a time in which awe and wonder were more present. The trouble with adulthood is that few of us can stand much awe and wonder for long. It reminds us, too often, of our distance from it, our necessary separation from the way things once were. Awe and wonder send us to the travel agent to book the first flight to Cancún or Acapulco, places that are mercifully less real than Oaxaca, places that are gorgeous and corrupt.

Color in Oaxaca has nothing to do with travel posters. I think of the hundreds of flies blackening the fresh red meat in the *mercado,* of the bees making the halves of squash yellower as they swarmed over them until it was hard to distinguish bees from the flesh of the squash. I think of the intricately woven blankets and shawls in which the Indians must have decided to send all colors to school to discipline them— the strict rows of color waiting for some final unraveling, and the blankets hanging there by the hundreds, each one a little different from the next. In childhood, all colors are indelible; they cannot be washed out. It is true that sometimes, in the bitter compromises of adult life, we think the truth of childhood is tiny; it is immense. It is one reason to feel bitter: "why won't the colors be the colors they once were? Why are the colors lying?" But in Oaxaca, for some reason, they do not lie. They are, like Paradise, what they were. And therefore they appear to be lying. A trick of light. But light is not a trick. Age is the trick that has been played on us. Looking may be an inexpensive pleasure, but there is, finally, a price to pay for all this innocent gazing—if only because no one remains innocent forever.

I have not yet said anything about the fire-eaters. In Las Vegas fire-eating is a cheap floor-show trick done with helium and it is relatively harmless. In Mexico, it is a different matter altogether, and not so pretty. The important thing for a fire-eater to remember is never to inhale. Islanded and seemingly cut off by the traffic on the medians of long boulevards in Mexico City, or across from those outdoor cafés surrounding the tree-shaded plaza in Oaxaca, where the strains of music drift from the military band assembled in the park, a young man fills his mouth with a solution of diesel fuel or gasoline, and then exhales carefully while holding a lighted coal approximately six inches from his lips. The exact distance, of course, varies with the individual artist. The age of each fire-eater varies as well, but not by much. I have never seen a middle-aged fire-eater. In fact, most give it up before they turn twenty. Those who do continue simply do not live long; or, if they live, they grow too inept to eat fire because the fuel itself, and the fumes, begin, as my friend Ernesto Trejo says, "to eat the brain." Some of the younger boys are lucky enough to acquire seared and puffy lips after only a couple of practice exhalations. That is, they are lucky enough to become scared. Most fire-eaters have to give it up when their sense of timing begins to slip. Again, the trouble has to do with the fuel itself. It is impossible not to get high on the fumes, and, if a boy gets high enough, or even if he reaches the same state of intoxication often enough, his sense of timing begins to fade ever so slightly. And too, if he is high, the chances increase that he will begin, for whatever reason, to laugh. Since in all laughter one must involuntarily inhale, not only the face and lips but also the inside of the mouth, the throat, and the lungs, will become momentarily aflame. There *are* stories of suffocation, but they are rare.

If you are among the very poor, the quickest way out of poverty is to get high, and, if you can, to stay high. And a fire-eater can get high and make money doing it. In the plaza at Oaxaca, if he works hard, a boy can earn perhaps five hundred to two thousand pesos for an evening's work. This amounts to anything from three to fifteen dollars a night, tossed in the tin can of the performer's younger sister as she weaves among the tourists drinking their margaritas or cappuccinos at the tables of the outdoor cafés—the Café del Jardín usually, or, less often, the Portal or the Café de la Reforma. For those sitting leisurely at those tables, there is always the exquisite view of the lighted park behind the flames. And when the acrid smell of burned diesel fuel or gasoline wafts back, someone orders another drink—perhaps coffee this time, and a glass of that harsh brandy, Fundador. Perhaps I even begin to fall in love with the woman sitting next to me, Elena, but then I remember she is Czech, and a Marxist, and she lives in Hamburg now. And that is far from where I live. When another flame goes up against the darkness, I reflect that nothing I have ever taken up with anyone else has lasted very long. Which is all right, finally, in the end; for it often takes a long time for things to come completely to an end between people.

It is all right, except that one of my friends is Martín, who owns the most beautiful smile in Oaxaca. His smile is rivaled only by that of his cousin Socorro, who sells gardenias that are always beginning to appear faintly discolored around the edges of their petals. She moves gracefully from table to table, balancing her basket on her head. Her smile is slier and slower to form, and it seems to blossom from some still place in her thought. It seems to come from a long way off. But Martín's smile is the smile of someone who seems always to be remembering how lucky he is to have been born at all, the smile of someone who has worked out all the odds against just such an event, and found them immeasurable. Once, after I took his picture, he looked me sternly in the eye and said that I owed him a *torta,* a tortilla filled with charbroiled meat, and then he smiled as if to say I owed him nothing. Nothing at all. His is the voluptuous smile of a swimmer breaking the surface of still water. I suppose I wanted it to last.

Martín shines shoes for a living. Or at least he did up until two weeks ago, before I left for San Cristóbal, where I stayed for two dollars a night beneath a cold rain that kept falling, and where I hiked to all the churches on the hills overlooking the rain-wet and shining city, and where nothing happened no matter whether I prayed or did not pray. The Café Olla Podriga was filled with French and American kids who chatted mostly about drugs and who seemed terribly gentle and uninteresting. I slept through the long bus ride back to Oaxaca, where Martín greeted me with his quick and good-natured laughter in the plaza that afternoon. It was then that he proudly held up his dark-green can of diesel fuel and his stick with its coal on the end. And so I lectured him in Spanish, carefully enumerating all the dangers. At last he told me politely but with some firmness to shut up, and then filled his mouth from the spout on the can and held up the lighted coal and signaled for a photograph. Which I took. Afterward Martín said the print ought to be worth at least a *torta,* and I reached into my pocket for the money.

That night I sat with Elena and my friend Scott, a filmmaker, while many of Martín's relatives and friends gathered around him in the street, opposite the Café del Jardin, to witness his debut as a fire-eater. Perhaps the only good thing anyone could say in my behalf is that I refused to watch him, although I could not help but notice, out of the corner of my eye, each flame that went up into the air. The show seemed to last a long time, then there were no more flames. At the table we all argued politics far into the night. No one agreed, and after a while Señor Ruiz turned the lights out in the Café del Jardin, and we stood up to say good-bye.

Some Notes on the Gazer Within

Poetics

When I began thinking about this a few months ago, I decided
that what I would not talk about was craft. As Mark Strand
states in a recent article in *Antaeus:* "[T]hese days with the
proliferation of workshops, craft is what is being taught."
Well, talking is teaching: when Sandra McPherson or Donald
Justice or Robert Hass writes about craft, such talk fascinates
me, and craft becomes, rightly, that most private of dialogues
between the poet and his language. But Strand is right, too.
Often my workshop at Missouri (especially the graduate work-
shop) is involved with prescribing remedies for poems—
remedies which have to do with the necessary, technical, and
not at all visionary work of repairing one line, or weighing, as
if in the palm of a hand, a caesura. Of course, I talk most
about poems that are *most* finished. Then the multitude of
formal decisions that are made are worth troubling over,
worth talking about. But I am, then, talking about technique:
when a poem is very poor, silence falls quickly, and there is
little to say about that poem. There may be a great deal to say,
however, about poetry itself, about the imagination, about vi-
sion. And I risk foolishness by talking about such subjects. I
know, really, that if I don't talk about it, someone else will. And
I may not agree with what he or she has to say. So I must either
talk about the imagination, or be silent.

Of course, there is that as an alternate, and even absolute,
stance; there is silence. Why say anything about the imagina-

Originally printed in *Field* 26 (spring 1982). Reprinted here from *A
Field Guide to Contemporary Poetry and Poetics,* ed. Stuart Friebert and
David Young (New York: Longman, 1982), 102–23.

tion at all? And if it is possible, after enough experience, for a poet to make generally correct formal decisions in the moment of writing a poem, why talk about poetics, about craft or technique? After all, the influence of a theorist like Pound has been deeply assimilated. Now, when most poets write, they do not have to admonish themselves: "Don't be viewy." They already know that they won't be, and for this they can thank Pound for having entered, inextricably, into their own poetry and into their very culture. Besides, couldn't there be something damaging to the poet, and something even unlucky, in trying to understand the principles of what must be, at some moments, a mysterious and sullen art? A poet as gifted as Margaret Atwood thinks so, or thought so in *Field* 4: "I don't want to know how I write poetry. Poetry is dangerous: talking too much about it, like naming your gods, brings bad luck . . . you may improve your so-called technique, but only at the expense of your so-called soul." As a notion about poetry and about the psyche, this states powerfully enough the fear that the soul can be lost simply by talking too much about poetry. I could expect then, that Keats and Eliot and García Lorca were damaged by writing about such ideas as "negative capability" and the "objective correlative" and "duende." And this is a possibility. But unless I am very superstitious about the early deaths of Keats and García Lorca, I could just as well believe that such ideas, in prose, helped the poets concerned, and helped their poetries, even when they broke the rules they made. It occurs to me also that one of the ways in which Pound entered our culture was by the public stridencies of his own criticism, his prose. That is, our century and our poetry didn't simply happen. Pound happened *to* us.

What interests me here is a deeper poetics, one that tries to grasp what happens at the moment of writing itself—not a discussion that indulges in prolonging what Marvin Bell has called the pointless "dualisms" of form versus content; nor a poetics that praises one kind of poem as *organic* while denouncing another as artificial. Ultimately, the trouble with such classroom determinations is that they do reduce poetry to technique, to something stripped of vision, something which gives the illusion of being soluble through *either/or* choices; they make poetry harmless. And in doing so, they lie.

We all know that poetry had better come, if not "as naturally as Leaves to the Tree," then at least with something more alive and luminous than a servile, cynic's technique. We know that a poem made to order from theory is slave labor, just as we also know that a poem, any poem, is artificial in one huge respect—if only because, as Eliot's character so famously complained: "I gotta use words when I talk to you."

Sources

But if this circumstance is true, where do poems come from? It seems to me that any poetry, any realized "making," comes almost directly from some kind of actual center, some location of energy. This morning, reading at random in *Pavannes & Divagations,* I found this in "Madox Ford at Rapallo," an interview:

> *Pound:* What authors should a young Italian read if he wants to write novels?
>
> *Ford:* (Spitting vigorously) Better to think about finding himself a subject.

Ford's exasperated (or mock exasperated) reply is simple and direct enough. But I would go further and stress, beyond the unwitting Ford, this: to find a subject is also, simultaneously and reflexively, the act and art by which anyone finds himself, or herself. A poet finds what he or she is by touching what is out there, finding the *real.* Yet the mistake I see made so often by beginning poets is that they want "to look into [their] hearts, and write!" But at nineteen a poet usually doesn't have much experience to depend on. When such poets write "from the heart" they often doom themselves to trite poems, to greeting cards full of clichés, or to poems that are truly and entirely subjective; that is, entirely incomprehensible. The best beginning poets I know are also the most literary: what they demonstrate is a love for poetry rather than a love for *themselves.* Let me exaggerate and be at once overly literal and the mind's peasant for a moment: to look into my heart is to look into a muscle. To really look inquiringly inward as Sidney advises or as the most well-intentioned guru advises is to encounter, at least on some very honest days, my own space; it is to discover how empty I am, how much an onlooker and a gazer I have to be in order to write poems. And, if I am lucky, it is to find out how I can be filled enough by what is not me to use it, to have a subject, and, consequently, to find myself as a poet. I like to oversimplify Husserl by saying: *Consciousness is always consciousness of something.* I am no phenomenologist, and I know that such a "something" is different from the simple materiality of the world that I mean, but here I have misunderstood Husserl just enough for him to be meaningful, meaningful to *me.* His remark becomes, in its way, as possible for me as George Oppen's lines: "Two. / He finds himself by two." And of course "he" does, or I do; and how else could it, and "I," have taken place at all: for example, that miracle of dawn or twilight along the road and me there, looking out of my skull, a witness to it? And this must occur many times, with regularity, or else the world would be nonsense, a mute noise.

Landscapes

What is "out there" is a world, a landscape. I don't know what could be more unfashionable just now than the whole "idea" of landscape, but at times, for me, the world *is* a landscape, and I think of my own poems as if *they* were landscapes, or as if I could refer to them by virtue of their places. A recent poem, for example, is spoken by a ghost on the banks of the Missouri River; another has as its focus a cemetery in Granada, in Spain; still another poem remembers an orchard and then remembers consequently a small, decaying California seaside resort with its stucco motel, once a coral red, fading to an almost thoughtful shade of pink. A poem I worked on last night is introduced by a few moths outside an asylum in a small town in Missouri, and earlier I was thinking of a line about a steel mill in Syracuse, New York, a place in which I once worked, and which was, I suppose, ugly and dangerous; its appalling, final meaning must be that republic of iron filings in the lungs of the men who have to work there. I did not, of course, praise the place in my poems. But it was human, a human landscape. I confess that the gazer inside me had a grave affection for the fire glaring in those furnaces from evening until midnight.

In fact, the landscapes I choose for my poems, often, have nothing to do with the landscape that surrounds me: when I look out my window I see my neighborhood, and I know that beyond it is a small, Midwestern university town. I find that I have very little desire to write anything about it, though its intimacy occurs, surely and obliquely, in my recent poems. But I wonder if my own neighborhood, some tract housing with lawns and trees, makes me uncomfortable as a poet. Do I merely choose asylums, steel mills, and cemeteries in García Lorca's birthplace out of personal morbid fascination and depravity? Maybe . . . but such an aesthetics would be at once sentimental and cynical, and my poems are still not much like *Baretta*. It could be that I choose painful subjects because such sterility, human sterility and loneliness, is part of so many modern landscapes. By this I mean the shopping mall, the suburbs, the business loops, the freeways and boutiques with cute names. They are all part of a modern reality that I would prefer to forget, or ignore. To most people I suppose such landscapes are slight, and unmenacing. To me they are the death of the landscape, and the eye's starvation. Therefore, the asylum, the steel mill, the cemetery, the ghost on the riverbank, the dying resort beside the unfading Pacific are locations, for me, of a human fertility within time.

But if any poet has tried, recently, to confront almost exclusively these most sterile landscapes, it is Louis Simpson in his two most recent volumes; his *Searching for the Ox* comes closest, I suppose, to that place where most of American living gets done, the suburb. And yet, the domestic crises detailed so beautifully, and documented with real grace in such poems as "The Stevenson Poster" and "The Foggy Lane" are poems of *wealthy* suburbs, and such wealth may be as necessary to Simpson's purposes as it is to John Cheever's. Yet even amidst such a setting, Simpson needs, if not Chekhov, at least the ghost of Chekhov's irony, and Chekhov's distance from his setting. All this affords Simpson's poetry its romance, and such a romance is just what the suburb needs; it needs to be soiled by the human. This is, by the way, an explanation and an admiration of Simpson, not a criticism. Who doesn't need Chekhov by now, and need him badly? To confront reality without a context, without this possibility of a romance, is, as Stevens phrases it, "to confront fact in its total bleakness." This is so, essentially, because a wilderness of tract homes is a world without imagination, and a world without imagination is a lie. Such a world tries to assure its inhabitants that there is no death, no passion, no vision. This is, I think, what prompted Zbigniew Herbert to say, jokingly one day as we were driving through South Pasadena and talking about architecture, that the only "solution" to Los Angeles was to burn it. There is an early, and brilliant, and even vicious poem by William Stafford which is eloquent about this world without imagination. After telling his readers, "We moved into a housing tract," Stafford, with all the proper rancor and customary modesty, closes his poem in an address to Bing Crosby, whose ranch he visits, accidentally, it seems, on his way west: "Every dodging animal carries my hope in Nevada. / It has been a long day, Bing. / Wherever I go is your ranch." Who would have expected Stafford to strike such a Marcusean chord, and to sound it so clearly?

In his essay "The Noble Rider and the Sound of Words" Wallace Stevens states that his phrase "the pressures of reality" means "the pressure of an external event or events on the consciousness to the exclusion of any power of contemplation." And though Stevens goes on to state that this is what the poet evades and escapes through the balance of his imagination which takes *in* reality, Stafford's poem remains firmly affixed by the pressure Stevens has described. Somehow, in its design, Bing's ranch is outside history, outside time; there are no deaths in the barracks of the suburbs, only disappearances. Outside time, the pressure of reality continues undiminished.

Such pressures and such landscapes have proliferated and become obstinate in recent years. Sometimes I believe that the one vast and wedded consciousness that was required to win World War II built, almost simultaneously, the tract home, the atomic bomb, and the Dixie cup. I am not, of course, saying much here that is genuine sociological news. But my interest is personal: I don't believe I can bear witness to such landscapes for long without feeling merely exhausted, drained, and spiritually beaten. In these place *I* must do all the looking, all the gazing. Because no one has ever died *into* such landscapes, it may be that no one can live in them, either; I don't know. I do know that as I watch my eyes pay enormous taxes while the gazer inside me dies for a few moments.

This death has something to do with time. Tract housing, most suburbs, malls, and shopping centers on the perimeter of any city or town seem to wish, in their designs, to be beyond time, outside time. To stare for three hours at a K-Mart is to feel myself rapidly aging, not K-Mart. And this is not an experience of my own mortality, either. It is only a way of feeling how that mortality can be insulted. And though I am not about to try to stare down any buildings, I do think of those who must work there, and of the alienation, even from themselves, that laboring in such places will make them feel.

Yet the authentic experience of any worthwhile landscape must be an experience of my own humanity. When I pass fields or pass the deserted streets of a small town in the Midwest at supper time, or pass avenues of closed warehouses I am not alone, I think. Someone or something has lived here; some delicate linkage is preserved between past and present. I am filled by, *looked at* by, the landscape itself; the experience is not that of a mirror's, but a true exchange, until even something as negligible as some newspapers lifting in the wind on a street, at night and before a rain, are somehow soiled by an ineradicable humanity, and by the presence of the dead, of the about to be born.

The Terrible World

And yet Williams is right: anything *is* a proper subject for a poem. To deny this is to deny a central tendency in American poetry today. But this is not what I am doing, of course. The essential problem is always the poet's not the theory's. I agree with James Wright that Williams was able to do what he did do because of the truculence of his vision, because of his character. Williams could use anything in the world as a subject precisely because the poet's imagination had contended so arduously with the pressures of reality (*The Desert Music* reaches the same conclusion as Stevens reaches regarding this) that Williams began to break down and demolish the bedrock dualisms that had kept Williams himself and the world the world. Consequently, the usable world, the broken bits of a green bottle lying between the walls of a hospital on cinders, held under the magnification of the poet's lyric, became an impersonal lyric, a lyric which the poet had evacuated. The poem was Williams's, of course; that is, he wrote it. But really, insofar as it was a moment, merely, of perception, it was everyone's moment. And that is its problem, its availability. One student, writing about the poem on an examination, said it proved that one could find beauty anywhere. Does it do that, and if so, should it? I believe, as Susan Sontag states, that good modern art looks back with a stare; it doesn't tell me what to feel or provide me with easy clues. But can a poem really stare back? Can words *be* things? Can they *not* mean? To what extent is my student's interpretation verifiable? Doesn't Williams tell us that the cinders are a place "where nothing will grow?" Is this poem both impersonal and corny? There is a way in which it may have taken all the lonely, later work of Williams, and the work of many of the best poets of our time, to recuperate the poet. This has been, I believe, one of the tasks of contemporary poetry—to recover the poet and the idea of the poet for our time. Such has been the constant example provided by such poets as James Wright, Anne Sexton, Philip Levine, Adrienne Rich, John Ashbery, Sylvia Plath, Mark Strand, and Margaret Atwood—to name only a very few who occur to me at the moment—poets who created the role and reality of the poet during the 1960s and 1970s. Yet it would be false to assume that this poetry has been concentrated wholly upon the Self, or exclusively upon the Self. In many ways it may have sought only to rescue poetry from some extremes, some abysses, of modernist impersonality. There may be a way in which the more contemporary poet has been engaged upon a recovery of an *idea* of a poet—so that his or her choice of subject reveals him or her *as poet.*

And certainly the pressure of reality exists externally for newer artists just as terribly as it did for earlier ones—or almost as terribly. I think against myself now and then, and think now of T. S. Eliot watching for German aircraft from the roof of Faber and Faber during the bombing of London, or of Pablo Neruda, who wrote of such pressures and of the power they had of embarrassing any motive for metaphor, or simile: "The blood of the children / flowed out onto the street / like . . . like the blood of children." Neruda in midstride suddenly realizes that to make poetry out of this circumstance is to endanger his own humanity, but he is too honest, and too terrible, to back down. As Stevens also noted, in his *Adagia:* "As the world grows more terrible, its poetry grows more terrible."

And yet the poets who have written of such a "terrible" world have done so, it seems to me, out of a memory of it, or at least at some distance from it. Or they have invented a subject through which such a world can be documented, felt, and reexperienced. Or they have introduced a new method or style into their poetry; a Japanese friend informs me that after Hiroshima haiku and tanka forms fell into disuse, and surrealism became the ruling aesthetic. Do such devices, such methods, bring the poet closer to the world or hold attention at a workable distance, or both? And what does anyone write *about* in such a world? That is, how do poets achieve that final invention, themselves?

Poetry and Animal Indifference

I'll only presume to answer, to attempt to answer, from my own experience, and from my own reading of others' experiences. My most frequent problem as a poet is to have no subject, to have "nothing at heart," an ailment that Stevens once defined as misery. The corollary to such misery is an extreme and moody self-consciousness, which of course prevents me from finding anything worth writing about. Once, after not writing anything worth typing up for a few weeks, I complained to a friend, a remarkable poet who is gifted with an unfailing intuition. His advice was simple; he said to try writing "about yourself at an earlier stage, or an animal." I wondered, then, why he mentioned an animal. Now I think I know why. Animals are objects of contemplation, but they are also, unlike us, without speech, without language, except in their own instinctual systems. When animals occur in poems, then, I believe they are often emblems for the muteness of the poet, for what he or she cannot express, for what is deepest and sometimes most antisocial in the poet's nature. The other thing that occurs infallibly when the poet places the animal in the world, or in the world of the poem, is the recovery of the landscape. It is no longer a world without imagination, or the world of tract housing beyond time. In animal poems the fox may live in the yellowing wood behind the service station; the hawk may be above the billboard. But if they are there, so is time there.

So many poets have written, recently, about animals that I don't feel now like making out a long and tedious list of them. What interests me is what the choice of such muteness suggests or openly testifies about poetry, and about the role of the poet. Seemingly, the poem sustains a paradox: the poet is *speaker*, of course, and yet the poet, evading the pressure of reality by a contemplation of the animal, also desires to express a mute condition. The poet wants to speak of, or to, or through, what is essentially so other that it cannot speak. The muteness or silence of the animal equals that of the poet. Perhaps there is some secret similarity between humans and animals, some desire to close the gap between species. Keats remarks, in passing, on this.

> I go among the Fields and catch a glimpse of a Stoat or a field mouse peeping out of the withered grass—the creature hath a purpose and its eyes are bright with it. I go amongst the buildings of a city and I see a Man hurrying along—to what? the Creature hath a purpose and his eyes are bright with it.

In his poem, "Horse in a Cage," Stanley Plumly notes how his father approaches a horse: "my father, this stranger, wanted to ride. / Perhaps he wanted only to talk." These instances, in which the poets note animals and humans sharing characteristics, are rare, however. And perhaps D. H. Lawrence's short poem about the youth and the horse attains the apotheosis of such contact—when the boy and the horse are "so silent they are in another world." They are rare not because the animals are not often given human characteristics, but because, in these examples, the role of the poet is extremely modest; the poet is never quite there, never blocking the poem. It is what Keats might have called, on a charitable day, "disinterestedness."

In many poems, of course, the animal is not natural, because in a poem the beast may be wholly imagined, and therefore altered from the prison of nature, and paroled, briefly, by the poem itself, and by the poet. And sometimes a poet chooses an animal because the poet is mute, and also because, as in the poem below, the poet is prophet.

They Feed They Lion

Out of burlap sacks, out of bearing butter,
Out of black bean and wet slate bread,
Out of the acids of rage, the candor of tar,
Out of creosote, gasoline, drive shafts, wooden dollies,
They Lion grow.
                      Out of the gray hills
Of industrial barns, out of rain, out of bus ride,
West Virginia to Kiss My Ass, out of buried aunties,
Mothers hardening like pounded stumps, out of stumps,
Out of the bones' need to sharpen and the muscles' to stretch,
They Lion grow.
                    Earth is eating trees, fence posts,
Gutted cars, earth is calling in her little ones,
"Come home, Come home!" From pig balls,
From the ferocity of pig driven to holiness,
From the furred ear and the full jowl come
The repose of the hung belly, from the purpose
They Lion grow.
                    From the sweet glues of the trotters
Come the sweet kinks of the fist, from the full flower
Of the hams the thorax of caves,
From "Bow Down" come "Rise Up,"
Come they Lion from the reeds of shovels,
The grained arm that pulls the hands,
They Lion grow.
                    From my five arms and all my hands,
From all my white sins forgiven, they feed,
From my car passing under the stars,
They Lion, from my children inherit,

From the oak turned to a wall, they Lion,
From they sack and they belly opened
And all that was hidden burning on the oil-stained earth
They feed they Lion and he comes.

Philip Levine's poem creates an entirely imagined beast, an unreal lion from the too real landscape. Against this place, the poet invents a voice which the Lion cannot, in its utter otherness, even recognize. As an imaginative act, this cat derives what power it has from the fact that it is unseen, and existent in an apocalyptic future. But it is a future produced by the dialectic of the present: the mute law of the Lion. The poet's tone is not really rancorous; it is not even avenging. Such preciously ethical positions have withered here into prophecy.

And such prophecy (or what Ginsberg once called "spoken loneliness") is Levine's American inheritance. In earlier poems he confesses that his "page is blanker than the morning skies," and that since he no longer speaks, he "goes silent among men." But such muteness was not the death of the poet at all, it was only preparatory and purifying. It was only the necessary immersion into voicelessness, the prophet's apprenticeship. So the poet who is "silent in America," who has "nothing" to say, becomes the most formidable architect of himself and his place and his community, though it is a community of the lost. The contemplation of such a Lion must have been, for this poet, an inward, anxious, and prolonged gazing. And an outward witnessing. To invent such a beast is to recover, simultaneously, its landscape, to appropriate all memories of such places, to find oneself.

Why do I admire this terrible Lion? Because, though it may stare back with a blank look, it will not lie; it will not be "reasonable." It is this *lack* of response, this honesty and taciturn otherness that fascinates me. Whitman noted this, but contrasted it almost satirically to human society, so that his leaf beginning "I think I could turn and live with the animals" remains a lyric complaint *about* human society, and only ostensibly about animals. But poem animals, like the Lion above, are something more contemporary, and something much different. They are entities without any specifiably inherited significances:

Bull or world that doesn't,
that doesn't bellow. Silence.
This hour's so huge. A horn or a sumptuous sky;
black bull that endures the stroking, the silk, the hand.

Beyond all the clichés about the bull, there is the bull Vicente Aleixandre includes here, an animal of possibilities which makes the hour "huge" rather than banishes time. It exists before it means, or can mean, anything. That *fact,* the mute bull, is the subject of the poem. In some way, that fact *is* the poem.

Ted Hughes suggests this even more clearly. For him, poems "have their own life, like animals, by which I mean that they seem quite separate from any person, even from their author, and nothing can be added to them or taken away without maiming . . . killing them." Hughes is fascinated by the indifference of the animals he chooses and by their power, which is like the poet's.

Thrushes

Terrifying are the attent sleek thrushes on the lawn,
More coiled steel than living—a poised
Dark deadly eye, those delicate legs
Twiggered to stirrings beyond sense—with a start, a bounce, a stab
Overtake the instant and drag out some writhing thing.
No indolent procrastinations and no yawning stares,
No sighs or head-scratchings. Nothing but bounce and stab
And a ravening second.

Is it their single-mind-sized skulls, or a trained
Body, or genius, or a nestful of brats
Gives their days this bullet and automatic
Purpose? Mozart's brain had it, and the shark's mouth
That hungers down the blood-smell even to a leak of its own
Side and devouring itself: efficiency which
Strikes too streamlined for any doubt to pluck at it
Or obstruction deflect.

With a man it is otherwise. Heroisms on horseback,
Outstripping his desk-diary at a broad desk,
Carving at a tiny ivory ornament

For years: his act worships itself—while for him,
Though he bends to be blent in the prayer, how loud and
    above what
Furious spaces of fire do the distracting devils
Orgy and hosannah, under what wilderness
Of black silent waters weep.

Hughes praises the "efficiency" and even the "genius" of the
birds' instincts and contrasts this, in the poem, to the doubtings
and "head-scratchings" of ordinary humans. And yet this in-
stinct is related to art and sometimes manifested in it: "Mozart's
brain had it." This may be the only poem in any language
in which Mozart shares something with the self-devouring
shark, and in which neither composer nor shark is afflicted with
anything as naive as ethics. Both are totemic and equated,
really, with the inhuman, the *other* which Hughes envies, and in
whose presence Hughes is terrified. The only general solace
offered to "a man" in the poem is that "his act worships itself."
And the acts, carving, writing, or the contextually moral "hero-
isms on horseback," are only a dismaying mimicry of both in-
stinct and heaven's or hell's "Furious spaces of fire." The only
way in which Hughes can come close to the innocence, indiffer-
ence and terrible perfection of his bestiary is by a persona, by
disguising himself as an animal, and finding himself and his
landscape shamanistically.

Increasingly, it becomes evident to me that poets are not fasci-
nated by what is, in animals, like humans. And certainly no
modern poet would be found sentimentally detailing such phe-
nomena. No. Poets thirst after what is pure and other and
inhuman in the animal, in the poem animal, anyway. D. H.
Lawrence's snake, for example, retreating from its drink of
water at Lawrence's trough is "thankless." The eyes of Eliza-
beth Bishop's fish in her famous poem "shifted a little, but
not / to return my stare." And Cesare Pavese, in "Atavism,"
writes of an inertly self-conscious adolescent who gazes after a
horse trotting by and admires, of all things, its nakedness: "It
seemed forever— / the horse moving naked and shameless in
the sun / right down the middle of the street." These animals
are thankless, or shameless, or unaware, and they are praised

for that. But this is very different from the ultimately ironic envy of Keats: "O for a life of Sensations over Thoughts!" Rather, in each example, the poet makes enviable that animal which is not him or not her. The animal stands for, if anything, its poem. Of course these are poems about animals as well, but somehow each animal is translated into something neither adequately a symbol nor, any longer, an undisturbed animal. Each beast, in fact, seems a criticism of what Hughes called the "general lifelessness" which surrounds all poems.

It is no wonder that such animals are often a source of fear; they may be too "alive." Robert Lowell's skunks, at the close of his famous poem, seem to represent a pure and disinterested instinct, which is incapable, unlike Lowell, of fear. And the bees in many of Sylvia Plath's poems are animals that inhabit an impermeable, somehow distant world. Otherness is what Plath avidly pursued, and she could, in some of her later moments of writing, feel that she could pick up her genius as if it were an instrument of some kind— as if it, too, were other, and in a late poem she could call words "indefatigable hooftaps."

But what happens if a poet should attain a kind of oneness with his animal, become it, however briefly, in a poem? This is what goes on in Galway Kinnell's poem, "The Bear." Strangely, the poet at the end of this poem is impoverished by his own revelation: "what, anyway, / was that sticky infusion, that rank odor of blood, that poetry, by which I lived?" As the poet Marcia Southwick has noted, if the animal means poetry, then by killing it the poet has effectually ended his poem, or the life of his poem. And she is right: it is all past tense; the poet's ability coincides and evaporates with his vision because he invades the animal. The experience, repetitive and regressive, which Kinnell dreams inside the bear offers the poet a spiritual access which is both liberating and appalling. What the poet learns is that the body of the bear is the body of the poem, of "poetry." Everything is made of words after all, and asleep, beyond anyone's will, words dream, as Gaston Bachelard says they do, just as intensely as the hunter in this fabulous poem. By restoring and broadening the senses this poetry does accomplish one thing—it ignores and bypasses the praised and envied animals of Hughes, what Kinnell would call the "closed ego of modern man." The poet in "The Bear" is really hunting a larger, buried self, a mute self. Therefore, when the poet and hunter journeys this outrageously, when he pursues the poem, the animal, this ruthlessly, it is as if the "unconscious"—accustomed to being lured out quietly and obliquely in poems, or present in personae, is suddenly and simply there: body alone inside a bear's body, both gestative and dead.

The Moment of Writing

But can a poet take on, if not the body of his or her animal, then at least its spirit? Can a poet imitate in mind the grace of an animal's body? James Dickey desires this:

> It seems to me that most animals have this superb economy of motion. The instinctual notion of how much energy to expend, the ability to do a thing thoughtlessly and do it right, is a quality I esteem enormously. I want to get a feeling of instinctualness into my poetry. How to do this linguistically is a difficult thing. That it can or should be done might be an illusion. But it fascinates me to try.

A "feeling of instinctualness" must be close to the kind of thing Hughes admires. And I remember Philip Levine once saying that a poem began, for him, with an almost "visceral" sensation, as if the poem, in its otherness, or what Levine called "the animals I am not," originated at once in body and mind and wanted to reject neither.

To acquire the "instinctual" in the qualified sense of its usefulness above is also, I believe, to perform at least one ancient and liberating act: it is to go beyond whatever shallowness inheres in the daily ego, to concentrate upon something wholly other, and to contemplate it—the Muse taking the shape, momentarily, of deer, mole, spider, whale, or fish. As the poet attends to these shapes, he or she goes, as Gary Snyder says, "beyond society." For some time now I have been puzzled by another notion of Snyder's in *Earth House Hold:* "Outwardly, the equivalent of the unconscious is wilderness: both these terms meet, one step further on, as *one.*" I suppose, therefore, that the real wilderness is, like the unconscious, what is unknown; and it is also, increasingly, what is meant by the term *nature*. Traditionally "wilderness" has had connotations of the unlimited, the unmastered, an inexhaustible source—and even now it remains the favored preserve of what, in nature, may be wholly *other*. So a poet, no matter what his or her subject may be, and no matter what the landscape, goes "beyond society." And so this is what happens at the moment of writing: the wave takes the shape of the fire. What is "out there" moves inside. The poet becomes threshold.

Gazing Within

To write poems that come back out again, into society, to write poems that matter to me, I must become, paradoxically at the moment of writing, as other as a poet as any animal is in a poem. Then true craft, which is largely the ear's training, can occur. Before this, my ear can hear nothing—or it plays back whatever rag of a tune it caught that day since its true desire and purpose is to thwart the world and hear nonsense, which it will do in the end. Unless this absorption into the other occurs, I am condemned to be immured within the daily ego, the ego that lives in the suburbs.

This was my problem when I began a long poem, "Linnets," in 1973. Basically, I had nothing to say—so I had to find a way to say that with finality, with a stare, with style. At least, this is what I thought, anyway. So I chose the least likely incident possible for a poem: my brother shooting a small bird with a shotgun in his adolescence, in my childhood. I thought that by choosing such a subject I would learn how to write about nothing at all, which seemed to be my lot. But then, as I mentioned earlier, I become exceedingly self-conscious when I am not writing. It is this that prevented me from seeing what I could write about, what subjects there really were, and how I could be moved by them, feel them. The more I thought about the absurd subject of my poem, the more possibilities it began to offer. To begin with, there was the bird itself, and the *story*. The more I thought about it, the more I forgot myself, the more I became immersed in the other. Luckily, I had problems right away, problems of form. I had to tell a story and establish it as a frame and do this quickly: it all took some thinking which may have saved me, suddenly, from myself. (Coleridge, in a journal entry on the boat to Malta notes some sailors teasing a bird on deck, a pelican, and scolds them in his handwriting. Then he remarks that it's not their fault: it's lack of thought that leads to lack of feeling. *Not* the other way around.) After deliberating, I fashioned the story into prose, where it belonged as a narrative, and cast it as a parable of sorts, or fable. But a fable with no values. Any ready-made significance would have made my poem pretentious, and silly. I quote below the second section of the poem, the fable of some kind of wild justice done to my brother.

But in the high court of linnets he does not get off so easily. He is judged and sentenced to pull me on a rough cart through town. He is further punished since each feather of the dead bird falls around me, not him, and each falls as a separate linnet, and each feather lost from one of these becomes a linnet. While he is condemned to feel nothing ever settle on his shoulders, which are hunched over and still, linnets gather around me. In their singing they cleanse my ears of all language but that of linnets. My gaze takes on the terrible gaze of song birds. And I find that I too am condemned, and must stitch together, out of glue, loose feathers, droppings, weeds and garbage I find along the street, the original linnet, or, if I fail, be condemned to be pulled in a cart by my brother forever. We are tired of each other, tired of being brothers like this. The backside of his head, close cropped, is what I notice when I look up from work. To fashion the eyes, the gaze, the tongue and trance of a linnet is impossible. The eyelids are impossibly delicate and thin. I am dragged through the striped zoo of the town. One day I throw down the first stillborn linnet, then another, then more. Then one of them begins singing.

One major lesson I had to learn was to become empty and dumb and trusting enough to write every day. For this I needed, at times, blind patience, no theories about art. I worked more or less steadily on the poem from March of 1973 to June of that year. I was, throughout, relatively untroubled about what the poem might mean to anyone, or what it should mean. One thing led to another, bird to bestiary:

Whales dry up on beaches by themselves.
The large bones in their heads, their silence,
is a way of turning inward.

Elephants die in exile.
Their tusks begin curling, begin growing
into their skulls.

My father once stopped a stray dog
with a 12 gauge, a blast in the spine.
But you can see them on the roads, trotting through rain.

Cattle are slaughtered routinely.
But pigs are intelligent and vicious to the end.
Their squeals burn circles.

Mice are running over the freezing snow.
Wolverines will destroy kitchens for pleasure.
Wolverines are so terrible you must give in.

The waist of a weasel is also lovely. It slips away.

The skies under the turtle's shell are birdless.

Certainly, the poem meant nothing very clear to me: it only
satisfied me, and in many ways I stopped caring about what it
meant at all. I only tried, as Forster said, to "connect. Only
connect." It felt better to connect than to know anything in
advance, and besides, what did I care if it made sense? The only
friend I showed the poem to in rough stages, David St. John,
was too kind to do much but praise it. What I wanted was to
write it; to feel myself become suddenly steeper and more
daring every day I worked on it. I say "steeper" because that
was how I felt or how it felt. I confess I don't remember much
of those moments of writing the poem—which is to say I don't
remember much of those months, or the days of those months.
I remember my desk, how the light would fall on it, the colors
in the room. It seemed to me that I could feel the almost
palpable solitudes inside the grain of wood in the desk, or
inside the ink in the fountain pen. Aside from that I was any-
one forgetting himself inside a task: the only other thing I tried
to do in the poem concerned craft. I tried to break a rule in
each section—do something I'd never done before. And that
was enormously pleasant. I'd begun to love going to the poem
each day, as a child loves going to a secret place, inhabited by a

secret love, speaking to that intimate No One. And after all, isn't the hermitage of the poem like that place. The words appear: the wave takes the shape of the fire: the trees turn green again for some reason. When I remember writing "Linnets" I see myself staring out at those trees, late at night, when they are illuminated by street lamps. I watch myself bend to the poem again. I am at peace.

At the High Meadow

In March the arthritic horses
stand in the same place
all day.
A piebald mare flicks her ears back.

Ants have already taken over
the eyes of the house finch
on the sill.

So you think someone
is coming,
someone already passing the burned mill,
someone with news of a city
built on snow.

But over the bare table
in the morning
a glass of water goes blind
from staring upward.

For you
it's not so easy.
You begin the long witnessing:
Table. Glass of water. Lone crow
circling.

You witness the rain for weeks
and there are only the two of you.
You divide yourself in two and witness yourself,
and it makes no difference.

You think of God dying of anthrax
in a little shed, of a matinee
in which three people sit
with their hands folded and a fourth
coughs. You come down the mountain.

Gazing within, and trying to assess what all this represents, I find I've been speaking, all along, about nature, about the attempt of the imagination to inhabit nature and by that act preserve itself for as long as it possibly can against "the pressure of reality." And by "nature" I mean any wilderness, inner or outer. The moment of writing is not an escape, however; it is only an insistence, through the imagination, upon human ecstasy, and a reminder that such ecstasy remains as much a birthright in this world as misery remains a condition of it.

An Interview by David Wojahn

I know you grew up in the San Joaquin Valley in California and its landscape has had a significant impact on your work, particularly on some of your more recent poems. Can you tell me about California, about your childhood there?

Well, I grew up on a farm where my father raised peaches, plums, grapes, and almonds. In some ways, as you get older, your childhood becomes more mythical in memory, and the place seemed almost idyllic there at times, although when I go back there I'm reminded that it was not in fact idyllic. But it's a very beautiful landscape: irrigated farmlands, and the Sierra Nevada mountains only an hour away; they rise up to nine or ten thousand feet from an elevation of about 250 feet; it's a dramatic landscape, incredibly hot in the summer and very mild in the winter.

How do you respond to California when you go back now?

The landscape I grew up in still looks as beautiful and as hopeless as it did then. I mean it always looks exactly like that: beautiful and hopeless. I grew up in what Joan Didion calls "the real California," where things are more resistant to change. Even if Fresno is now a huge sprawling town, it's essentially unchanging.

I ask these questions because your poems are often very focused on a particular landscape or locale, yet the speakers and personas of your

---

This interview was conducted sometime in 1982, possibly in Columbia, Missouri, or in Iowa City. Levis and Wojahn were friends and colleagues and, at that time, as far as we can surmise, Larry would have been working on the material that would later become the poems in *Winter Stars*. The various readings alluded to here would probably have been occasions for sharing these poems with an audience, perhaps for the first time.

*poems always seemed exiled from the places that are important to them.
I'm thinking of some of the poems in* The Dollmaker's Ghost *such as
"Picking Grapes in an Abandoned Vineyard" and "The Ownership of
the Night."*

Well, I guess I feel that way, or that my life has taken that
particular path of flight away from that location, from that
place; or else I feel exiled from it in some way. You go along
and what happens to you happens to you. You wind up in
strange locations and towns and even apartments for all sorts
of reasons that you can't figure out. I grew up in a house
which my family has owned since the Gold Rush, and I only
left our farm when I was eighteen and went to college in
Fresno, which I thought was a really big city. That sort of
upbringing has a lot do with how I think of myself. If you
moved around from place to place when you were a child you
no doubt have a more sophisticated perspective about home.
For example, I went to a little schoolhouse where there were
only three people in the first grade: there was Ronnie Barker,
a girl named Margery Elm, of all names, and myself. It was a
three-room schoolhouse, so they had the first and second
grade in the same room; they had a real bell on a rope that the
teachers would ring. My grandmother once taught there in
the 1890s. So there was a sedimentary layer of a family that
had been in that place for a long time, at least by California
standards. I saw *few faces.* The school was so tiny—there were
only about thirty-five people in it—that when neighboring
schools would come in to compete in athletic contests, I was
always struck by the variety of faces that could exist. I didn't
think that there could be such an incredible array of eyes,
faces, and bodies: I remember, actually, thinking just that as a
child. It was wonderful that there were so many certain faces;
but how could they exist? They were so out of place, shocking,
strange. So obviously I was an incredibly sheltered child. I
would just stand there marveling, watching people get off the
bus. The naïf of all naïfs. I'm not proud of this sort of upbring-
ing. I would never argue for it. To the Mexican Americans or
to the Armenians or to the Japanese or the Filipinos, I must
have been, as an adolescent, just another dumb Anglo.

*Do you think there's anything cathartic or therapeutic about your
obsession with ghosts, especially in the last book? I mean both the*

ghosts from your own personal past and the imaginary pasts of others.
Sometimes I feel that the difference between, say, your persona poems
and those of someone like Norman Dubie is that somehow you seem to
write about your characters because to do so is the only way to free
yourself from them.

That's probably true. For me, the ghosts are also ways to talk
about parts of myself that I wouldn't feel decent talking about
from the first-person point of view. I don't feel brave enough to
talk about them in the first person, or I felt too modest at a
certain point in my life to talk about them as if those parts were,
in fact, me—even if in fact they may have been me. There is
something different, of course, about the method of Norman's
poems. His are personae poems, and are often based on real
historical figures. My figures are often imagined or else they're
anonymous and private. His use of persona is more definite or
precise. The voice doesn't change or become, too overtly, Nor-
man's. It isn't as *violated* as mine.

I guess that leads me to my next question, which is how does this
personal, autobiographical self, which is portrayed in your poems, and
the imagined selves—all of your characters and personae—how do
they interact? I think of poems like "The Blue Hatband," and your
poems about Hernandez and Herbert—it's almost like we see this
speaker's self-conscious and private voice give way to a more selfless
voice that seems almost beyond the self of Larry Levis, more like a
medium or an adopted mask.

Well, the Herbert poem came from Herbert himself, who
was a friend of mine for two years when he taught at the same
place I did, California State University, Los Angeles. The Her-
nandez poem I wrote because I admire a number of his poems
and I've always sympathized with him: he was just a shepherd
kid from Orijuela who went to Madrid, which was eventually
the scene of his great triumph. His life was particularly mov-
ing: his first book was ignored, he fought in the Civil War, and
when he was imprisoned by Franco after the war he grew sick
and died. I'm attracted to his openness to both ecstasy and
misery. To me that was exceptional, and very touching. One
poem I've always wanted to translate was one in *El Ultima*
Riñcon, "The Last Loner." In it he's both tired of living and
overwhelmed with loving. It's actually a very Keatsian poem,
in which he implies that he is *too* happy, *too* fulfilled. And it

ends with some breathtaking lines, "Despues del amor, la tierra. / Despues de la tierra, nadie," which means "After love, the earth. / After the earth, nothing, no one." So I was thinking about those lines and I tried to write a poem for him. The Akhmatova poem came into being after I read D. M. Thomas's introduction to his translation of her poems, in which he tried to contextualize her writing in terms of her son getting locked up and the political events she lived through. Writers such as Herbert and Akhmatova lived in a world that is much harder than the world is for most American poets right now, though it could get harder at any moment.

Do you consider yourself to be principally an elegiac poet?

I often feel that that's what I *am* as a *human.* I would like to explore other areas; I would like to write a really funny poem, a poem of wit. But I really don't know how to do that yet. Also, it seems to me, or has seemed to me for a long time, that the elegiac poem, the poem that is meditative and narrative, simply touched me more deeply. Yet I agree with Roethke when he said that a poet should try to show as many sides of himself or herself as he or she, in all decency, can.

One thing about a lot of the Ghost *poems that is striking to me is that, as you've said, you've given a voice to people who wouldn't have had a voice otherwise. Sometimes I think, too, that many of your poems since* Dollmaker's Ghost, *which focus very heavily on memory, are similarly elegiac. They're trying to capture a past that's always elusive, always decisively lost.*

Well, some of them are overt elegies, for example four poems for my father, who died about a year ago—died hard, of Parkinson's disease. I guess one's own parents' deaths are difficult to think about. I can tell you I *did* when my father died, but I can't explain. I think you go a little crazy. At one point I was totally crazy. My father was cremated, and my sister and I had to drive into Fresno, going in to get this box of "ashes"—that's what they're euphemistically called. I knew it would be heavier than simple ashes, but I think my sister imagined they would be light and waferlike, and that her father had been transformed into a dandelion. Actually, the box was quite heavy, and I remember driving and making sure I didn't tip the box over, which *was* heavy, so as not to disturb her any more than she was already disturbed. I remember coming out into this hot Fresno street, and you know it's a Western city with all that awful Soviet Realism architecture—it looks as bad as Phoenix. And I'm walking out with this box of, you know, bits of bone, grease for the wheels of heaven, and ashes, and part of me is thinking about poetry. I hate to say this because it will seem cruel, but the secret of poetry *is* cruelty. Part of me is always a poet, still observing, still trying to put things together and unify—and I was blasphemously thinking: "This moment is probably going to be important, what you notice is going to be important." What I noticed was an overweight woman in a T-shirt walking her springer spaniel on the street and her T-shirt read, "K109 Rocks Out in Chicago!" and I couldn't get the incongruity of it out of my head. It wasn't incongruous, really. It was just my life, not a poem. I almost hasten to quote James Wright here: "I don't say it was a good life. I say it was a life." So some of the new poems are elegies; some of them are love poems. Sometimes you have to address things that are happening in your life that you really don't clearly understand and that's difficult. All the new poems I write are *me;* no personae.

What do you think then is the purpose of elegiac writing, of the ritual gesture of mourning that your poems seem to enact? Is there any kind of redemption or renewal that your concern for loss enables you and your readers to experience?

I don't know what the *result* of that concern is. Merwin, for example, has a wonderful circumspection of mind and charity in a little poem called "Elegy." He says, "who would I show it to?" which is, of course, the whole truth. Many times elegies are self-reflexive, and they often point not to the figure gone but to the person writing them, and they are meant to reveal that mind, that nature. But I think maybe it's in the century, too. You know, I've noticed it's not only in my poems but in many poems in America now that are elegiac. The poet James Moore wrote about this phenomenon recently and suggested that, because our culture is moving on toward the end of the century, it doesn't any longer have—except in rock 'n' roll music—any kind of raucous fantasia of youth. Poetry is always so *old;* everything else seems so young. Medicine is young; rock 'n' roll *seems* young; poetry? You read Ovid, you read Ben Jonson, Baudelaire, Dante, Villon, and they're young. But there's something elegiac in the whole fabric of our time, about which I can do nothing; the time in which I'm born is something *done to* me; it creates a particular style of thought, and a particular violation of the self, about which one can do nothing. That's not so bad: I mean, I'm actually happy to be alive in this age. I think I'd be overjoyed to be alive in *any* age: it's better than the alternative. I think we'll all find out. But I think there's something in our cultural fabric, a feeling of things which is profoundly elegiac and fin de siècle. Yet there's also another stance in poetry which has surfaced, one that's more ironic: Ashbery's work, with its combination of seriousness and wit within an individual poem, is a good example of it.

I guess all these questions are circling around a question. And that is, why do you write?

I write, first, for myself. I was talking to my wife last week, from whom I'm separated for now, and she was saying, "Why? Why this, why that?" She would say in letters, "You're still writing. You write all the time. Just keep writing," and I would reply, "I'm afraid if I stop I won't do it anymore." And she said, "Well, why? What are you afraid of?" And I said, "Well, writing keeps me feeling good about myself, keeps me feeling alive, keeps me . . . ," and then I said, "It's the only thing that keeps me interested." And she said, "Yeah. You said it—*I* didn't." Suddenly everything comes back and it's at once crystal clear and also meaningless: that tree disguised in shadow in summer, sunlight on a doorstep that transforms it into a threshold of desire and then of loss, just the pure phenomenon. Sex has an *x* in it because the lover's cross just *there* and forever, and that letter, that character, has, in itself, no meaning, and no sympathy or mercy. And we're stilled, bewildered by those people who are truly happy *all the time,* who have a cash box for a heart or have a little wizened raisin far too small to contain one. Almost everyone else has an enlarging kernel of doubt.

Do you find the process of writing to be painful, or is it pleasurable? Sometimes the very starkness of the subject matter is so chilling to me that I can't help but feel that your releasing that poem must have been sort of an agonizing process. Yet in that essay of yours, "Notes on the Gazer Within," you talk about how the times when you sit down to write a poem are those rare times when you're at peace.

I am at peace, at least during the moment of composition.

The thinking has to get done, it seems to me, before I sit down to write. Yet writing, obviously, is about discovering something in the *act* of writing, as Robert Creeley said. But if you were just flat out weeping or crazy or ecstatically laughing, it would be difficult to make the pen move. I want to give you a very high-toned, intellectual answer. But it is also like *Garp* where the kid shows the story to the woman he's about to marry and she's in tears and she says, "That's the saddest story I ever read." And *he's* leaping up and down with joy! Yes, there's emotion involved there, but it seems to me it's emotion that has been distilled, made palatable, pungent with its loss and with history, a myth. In readings I always end up including poems that I know might be frightening or depressing to people, but I never feel like changing or altering them. I've always thought the truth was hard.

How do you sit down to begin a poem?

Well, I begin by listening to music. I make a pot of coffee, I might have a drink, and I put on something, usually jazz, but sometimes rock 'n' roll, sometimes classical. It is important to listen to the best performers—Perlman, Gould, Stern, et cetera. And I listen for awhile and I doodle for a while; sometimes I draw pictures. Usually everything begins with a letter, with a syllable: often it's the "k" sound, I don't know why. Must be infantile. Donald Hall says sounds in poetry satisfy infantile pleasures; *I'm* probably saying "caca" all the time. But I'll leave that diagnosis to Erikson or Piaget. Just a sound, a little phrase, that you might want to translate over into something else, to take it from that into words, into a musical phrase. And that's harder to get into English, since we have an inflected language. It's a language that seems to me less musical than Spanish, for example . . . I begin to get a few lines and then the whole thing begins to form. Then I'll cross out things that seem coarse, bad, overly conceptual, convoluted; but I do try to get a first draft at one sitting. Then I spend a week or two tracking down the alternatives. That's what's really fun, of course: just going and seeing where it goes.

How long does the process of revision take?

Oh, a few weeks. Sometimes less: sometimes only a week, it depends on how many problems, formal difficulties, a poem presents. I don't essentially measure a meter unless I'm openly working in one. Grammar is music. Everything is in the sound, the syntax, *the* grammar. When I revise I listen to the music of the thing. That's what I do—I listen. I listen very closely.

In the poems of Dollmaker's Ghost *and those poems since then, your concerns have been increasingly narrative and apply techniques that we usually associate with fiction. Have you ever tried writing fiction?*

No, I tried it once, wrote two pages and started laughing. I kept worrying about rhymes, about—as we have to in poetry, we have to keep rhymes out unless we want to *use* them because the language is so irresponsible and the tradition is so full of rhymes that the quirkiness of your own mind will offer a funny commentary on it, like a first violinist challenging a new conductor on his knowledge of *very technical* matters. In fact, if I try to write fiction, I am afflicted by the dreck and wreckage of the past, by a narrative and classical poetry. Well, I kept trying to keep rhymes out and I thought, "This is ridiculous—people writing fiction don't even worry about this." Of course, that's wrong: they probably *do,* you see. They're just used to writing longer, much longer patterns so they're worrying about this dialogue, or this way out; and the slings and shifts, it seems to me, are much larger. If you write long poems, you can sort of feel the larger slings and shifts of the language. And it is *so* exciting. I was thinking of writing a book of prose called *The Autobiography of a Totally Harmless Person,* but then didn't do it. I told Mark and Jules Strand the title, and they said; oh, it won't work; the title's not catchy enough. They said: why don't you call it *The Autobiography of an Evil Man?* And we all laughed, because humor is so right and so wrong and always unmerciful and decidedly social.

I'm interested in the movement of your work from a style that in The Wrecking Crew *and even in* The Afterlife *was very much influenced by surrealism, particularly Spanish surrealism—we've talked about that; Lorca and Alberti and Hernandez—toward a more meditative, narrative stance in* Dollmaker's Ghost. *I know a number of poets in your generation have made a similar move, and it seems to me that somehow your poems exemplify that shift most prominently.*

Actually, I was most influenced by marvelous American "surrealists"—if they can be called that: by Bly, Simic, Tate,

Lux, Knott. Yet I saw, at one point, that if I kept trying to write these little jewel-like poems that were composed almost entirely of images, of exquisite pleasure, that it reduced what my poetry was or could be. And then I thought the life of poetry, as it sustains itself or grows or renews itself, depends on incorporating into a poem that which I didn't think *was* poetry. Think about Frank Bidart; he appears on the surface to have no ear, no sense of breaking a line, yet everything, it seems to me, is done with incredible care. It's a matter of admitting other forms, other kinds of things into the province of poetry; otherwise, poetry has to exist on a diet that is too rich, too sculpted down to one narrow, little cavern into which it's always in danger of falling into the abyss of *utter* language. You can see that happening to the poets of the sixties. I love to write images, but what fascinates me about experience or about how I think of myself is something that I can't explain through images; it instead comes through a story or an anecdote. There was a certain point, when I was studying at the University of Iowa, when we all became aware of that. Between 1972 and 1975 I studied with Tess Gallagher, Laura Jensen, Marcia Southwick, Denis Johnson, David St. John, Norman Dubie, Michael Ryan, Michael Burkard, Michael Waters, John Skoyles, Elizabeth Libbey—and we were all finding new ways to do things. We came to Iowa at a time in which the image had already been so perfected that in some unspoken way we all understood that our energy had to move toward something else. I don't think at that point we were aware of its *being* that. Obviously, Norman Dubie, with his energy and generosity, had a great deal to do with it in many ways, and his intelligence was a stove for us all to be warmed by. David St. John suddenly, and I think more sharply than anyone, changed from being an imagistic poet to one capable of sweeping narratives and abstract meditations. This change was happening in a lot of other places, too. I guess I *couldn't* write an imagistic poem as well as Simic, or Bly, or James Wright (although he's not necessarily, it seems to me, an imagist) and, I thought, "Why do it, why try to do it, why play the game with these absolute wonders, who seem to do it so effortlessly and naturally?"

Well, what do you think now might be the limits of the narrative or meditative mode?

Oh, I don't know. Probably, now, self-parody. You want to avoid poems in which all it sounds like is that you're trying to write like yourself. And yet, on the other hand, I think of a poet like Simic: I'll buy his books forever. I love to read those kinds of poems. I don't care whether he ever changes or feels like changing: he needs to change about as much as Wilbur—that is, not a bit. I think that what he does is so fresh and so interesting, so authentic that I would never suggest, "Move on," because of a particular aesthetic position. I don't think one should *have* aesthetic positions. I think the process of deciding what one has to do is usually a natural one.

Does the recent interest in a kind of narrative poetry have anything to do with a renewed interest in writing poems in traditional form, traditional meter? One reads a lot of, say, sestinas, in magazines today, and that's a form that seems to invite meditative and narrative concerns if it's going to work—and I know some of your more recent work is in blank verse or in syllabics.

Yeah. I've written syllabics and blank verse and, well, the other day I wrote a poem in five-beat quatrains. I wanted to make sure I could still do it. When I began writing I wrote for two years in traditional meters—pentameter and blank verse, tetrameter, trimeter, syllabics. By casting something a blank verse line, you can make uninteresting language suddenly a lot more interesting—if only because of that slight pickup in rhythm. I don't think meters need to be used in that way, but I am saying that the ear deserves some respect. Yet I also think we ought to define form in a much broader way. I think Williams has been important, and Creeley and Olson, too, as people who broadened our ideas about form. I can't see any reason to rush back to a formal measure with rhyme unless one really feels that one can do something in a renewed capacity in the way that, say, Hart Crane did it in his poems. Or as Hugo did, or Philip Levine. The best recent formal verse I've seen comes from Gjertrud Schnackenberg—who employs form very strictly. But I guess I'm more interested in the people who are idiosyncratic masters of form—like James Wright, or more classical masters at it like Donald Justice and

Richard Wilbur. I think Justice always used the form and did not let the form use him. That's a real difference. I can't see using formal verse and saying, "Here's the answer." A lot of the formal poems I've seen—the bad ones—remind me of bad formal verse in the late fifties. I see no reason for that era to be revived.

Do you think some of the change has to do with anything political? A lot of the renewed interest in traditional verse came about the same time that the Reagan administration came into power.

I think it's difficult to say if something occurs because of a political reason or not. I think Reagan coming to power is a symptom of cultural malaise, and it has to do with high inflation and homeowners being worried and all sorts of other things that seem symptoms of other problems, mostly economic ones. But the new formalism came about, I think, simply because there are so many poets now that some people feel that they have no way of discerning anything clearly anymore. So they want to go back to something *measurable*, and that's what meter means: measure, from the Greek, right? They also wished to move against the charlatan flatness which they associated with the American idiom. And no matter what else you can do, if you can write in a pentameter, a hexameter, a trimeter, a tetrameter line, you are at least doing *something*. Such people, feeling insecure for good reason, might think, "Well, at least I'm doing *that*." I think Robert Hass in his essay on form is probably right in saying that free verse has been used so often that it's lost its cutting edge against formal meter, its adversarial position which once offered it so much energy. When you break a rule in poetry, it can give your poem a vast energy. But those rules have been broken too often, merely and timidly, often just for arbitrary and idiosyncratic reasons. When people go back to writing in meter now, they think they can find some new sort of energy. They may be right, providing that the five centuries of wisdom and craftsmanship that have gone into the making of the meter don't overwhelm them; they have to do something *new* with the tradition, as Hart Crane and Wallace Stevens did. One can't feel *very* proud of a poem written in quatrains with a particular rhyme scheme if all it does is sound like something written by one of the worst students of Yvor Winters or the worst poets in

New Poets of England and America. Who wants to go back to the Eisenhower era? Still, Winters could teach those meters, and who can do that now? Probably only Justice, Coulette, and Snodgrass. And who can teach you to renew that music? Only *you.* I'd like to define form in a way that's more expansive than the ways in which we've thought of it before, but we can't if we're thinking of measure or meter alone as form. It is and it isn't. I mean, if we enlarge it, let's think of form as rhythm that goes on and on over time. Many of the most basic English rhythms and rhyme schemes, such as a four/three line, characterize a lot of rock 'n' roll and New Wave music; but what a great gap there is between, say, Laura Jensen or Jorie Graham, and the Clash or the Jam. I mean, in a way, we've already *done* New Wave in poetry. We've already had poems that were like a burlesque of earlier poems, and yet also a renewal of the old traditions in poetry. There's a way in which we don't need it.

I'd like to ask you about your use of the line. The other night you were talking about Jarrell's capacity to push a ragged line to its limits, and I sometimes feel that you deliberately roughen up your lines through varying line lengths and unexpected enjambments. Few of your lines seem predictable, yet they generally seem right. What's the purpose of that technique and how do you go about working on that strategy?

I think in the case of *Dollmaker's Ghost,* I had an idea that I wanted a kind of linear energy—something that went *across* a line. But I also wanted a kind of vertical energy to move down through the poem, thanks to the way in which the stanzas were shaped. One of the things that helped me to do this was a particular kind of enjambment, a violent runover of the line. But they're not enjambments so violent that the reader can't sense my pause at the end of the line. I want the individual lines to always keep a certain integrity. To capitalize the letter of each line also helps to draw attention to that fact, helps to say that it's still a line and not something arbitrary. A line is what *time* says to you, in the intimacy of terror; it's something in your ear when you think you're just driving home. At a certain point in writing *The Dollmaker's Ghost* I was very aware of the shape of the poem, the way it looked on the page; aware in some sort of silly little way of how important that shape was to me. So much happens in the heat of composition, at least in free verse, and it happens so quickly that I often feel that lines may be broken in the heat of that moment. But at the same time I feel that the line establishes itself as a distinct unit—it becomes almost like a dance step.

How do you know when a poem falls into a stanzaic pattern?

I think it announces itself pretty clearly and pretty early for me. I find it difficult to go back and place a poem into stanza form after I have done a rough first draft. It always seems to announce itself in the first draft. You need to stay out of the poem's way and be smart enough to get rid of your preconceived ideas about what you want to have happen. The poem you're writing, your own luck, and your subconscious may know more than you do.

One very distinctive aspect of your work is a quirky use of punctuation. Dave Jauss calls it a "preponderance of punctuation." There are a lot of internal caesuras in the line that are the result of commas that aren't grammatically necessary, a lot of dashes, that sort of thing. What is the purpose of these techniques?

A lot of times I think the caesura is done for dramatic effect. I'm not disparaging that as a term—you know, I think dramatic effect is important in art. When you see ballet dancers move across a floor, you are aware of sudden stops, caesuras or pauses in the body that don't seem quite natural and yet on second thought they seem to be very artful. That line of them going across a floor becomes something more sensuous than it was before by virtue of stopping, of moving very quickly and then suddenly slowing things down as if there's as much pleasure and sensuousness in slowing down, in stopping and then going on, as there would be in simply moving very rapidly. I think that's something I had in mind—conceiving the line as a kind of body moving through time and space on the page. I was not thinking of that consciously, just feeling it, feeling that capacity to hurl forward and then, suddenly, quickly and briefly stop. So much has to do with music, you know. The particular music you're hearing.

How about shifts in diction, shifts in tone? I frequently see your work alternating between a kind of colloquial language and a more abstract kind of diction, also between a kind of high seriousness and a kind of black humor. Those extremes often operate within a single poem. Ashbery does that a lot, Marvin Bell does that. For example, a section of the new long poem you read last night, "A Letter," contains a long erotic passage followed by another passage that is densely metaphysical, but bridged by the statement, "To fuck is to know." This seems to be a good example of what I mean.

In that poem I wanted to try and talk about sex and, well . . . it seems to me that one could not know what one knows in this century and make a charmed case for sex being the answer to all the riddles of life. Lawrence and cummings tried that and did as well as anyone to try to make one recognize that; and you *do* recognize it to some extent, in culture and history and also in one's own life. But sex seems to be so many different things: it can be awful, it can be ecstatic, it can be boring. There's a cynicism in that poem, but it's essentially a poem of praise for the erotic. I wanted to get all that down and I thought that one way to write that poem was to get everything to conform almost monochromatically to a certain level of diction. A poem like that inspires our trust because we feel it's by a poet with a steady life doing one thing well. I was thinking about that. The influence of Ashbery on my diction in that poem is also impossible to neglect or ignore—as is that of Levine in his most imaginative book, *One for the Rose*. . . . It seemed to me one can move easily from certain levels of diction or even themes or considerations about all this just by simply fusing things together. It might look disquieting in terms of the shifts things make, but that's all right, too: one could have art that would make someone slightly anxious or could put them off as well as comfort them. An earlier draft of the section you're speaking of was spoken by a dead ancestor of mine, a woman who became more and more interesting as she began speaking—but who in fact could not have said the things that are said in that section, such as "To fuck is to know." So I thought, well, that's really what *I'm* saying: I took the poem away from her, partly because I didn't want to embarrass her.

This brings me to my next question. Peter Stitt wrote a review of Dollmaker's Ghost *in* Georgia Review *that, at one point, criticizes the book because he doesn't believe you can actually know enough or care enough about the people you describe or the personas you adopt: you seem to know too much, to be too omniscient. How would you respond to that accusation?*

Oh, that. Well, there were a couple of people I wrote about in "Magnolia," the poem which he talks about. They in fact become junkies; they were friends and I did not think it would be right for me to describe them so specifically that others would recognize them. I felt wary about doing that; their lives are difficult enough; I feel wary about it now, as well. Yet I had to fictionalize some parts of their stories if I were going to be able to sympathize with them. The only hesitancy, the only remaining embarrassment I have about the poem has little to do with Stitt and has everything to do with what could be mistaken as admonishment at the end of the poem—which I do not think they would care for and which I do not care for at all. I don't care for giving moral lectures as Stitt does, and if the poem does anything like that, I'd be embarrassed. I mean, I liked those people. Their problems were enormous—that's all. It's sad to see it happen. But it happens, but "right and wrong" becomes in some cases a little naive.

The final poem in The Afterlife, *"Linnets," and "A Letter," the poem you read last night, are both long sequences. How do the longer poems differ from some of your shorter efforts. How does that earlier poem, "Linnets," differ from your newer one?*

Well, "Linnets" is much more imagistic and much more concerned with the natural world; it's a parable poem in which my brother shoots a linnet and there's a strange retribution for doing all this. It is, I guess, like shooting an albatross, though on a much smaller scale, I'm sure. So, anyway, the poem's all tied up in a kind of little myth. I think it differs from "A Letter" in that way, in that it has a mythical or hermetic method behind it, although you can say that about "A Letter" too; since the quoted thing from Ovid is spoken by Orpheus when he's petitioning the gods to descend to the underworld. He wants to go down to find Eurydice and bring her back, and there are little clues there about never looking back at each other as they *descend from* cliff dwellings. So those things are used, but in another sense "A Letter" is simply a love poem; it isn't playing elaborate games. Those games are interesting, but I just wasn't thinking of such things. I wasn't in that particular frame of mind.

One thing that seems to distinguish The Afterlife *poems from* The Dollmaker's Ghost *and some of the more recent poems is that there's a kind of mythic stance, mythic concern or manipulation of the archetypes in the earlier book that you don't see in the later one.*

Maybe one has to choose between history and myth. A lot of the poems in *Dollmaker's Ghost* are concerned with people who actually lived, such as Hernandez or Zbigniew Herbert or Akhmatova; and I think you would feel—at least with those people or even with Kees or those two men, Tea and Angel, two men who picked grapes and did a lot of other things out in Fresno—I would feel that a mythic texture brought in or imposed upon them would simply violate any dignity they ever had. What a figure like Akhmatova asks you to do is simply not to falsify her life, nor to falsify history itself. If you tried to make her into a myth, it would look literary in a bad sense. Of course, myth is so ancient and so large that anybody who is a real mythologist could see it everywhere; I have friends who in fact do that. Of course, they're often Greek and they often teach comparative literature and they've read everything under the sun. The daily is mythic to them.

How do you go about structuring a collection? I know that both The Dollmaker's Ghost *and* The Afterlife *seem to follow an arrangement that makes each book grow more assured in its vision as it comes to its final sections. Few individual collections I can think of seem to be constructed as carefully.*

Afterlife fell pretty casually into place. I wanted to have a strong beginning section and then a kind of interlude or meadow in the middle with shorter poems and more quietly lyrical movements. And I knew I wanted the long poem to come at the end. *The Dollmaker's Ghost* was a real problem, as I remember: a problem not only in arrangement but in poems, of knowing what to include. I sent the book to a friend, Daniel Halpern, to see what ideas he had about arranging it. I had some short poems that I kept out of that book, and Dan said something like, "Well . . . it's fine, but you have one peak after another here. No reader can take that for long. No reader should want to take it." And he was absolutely right, I thought, so I put the shorter poems back in, poems like "Truman, Da Vinci, Nebraska," "A Story," and a number of others; and I put them back in at points where they would lessen the action. I mean, even though we know people don't pick up poems and read them page 1 through page 72 or something, it's still important to have a strong continuity in the book. So I put the short poems back in, and other things, too. There's a little Weldon Kees poem that fit in with other things I was working on, though it is essentially different in style. The final thing that happened was when I met with my editor at E. P. Dutton, Jack MacRae, whose only suggestion was to move the poem "Picking Grapes in an Abandoned Vineyard" to the beginning of the book because he thought it a strong poem, and that the book needed a powerful opening.

Who, excluding contemporary writers, has influenced you?

Well, Eliot, when I was a kid, when I was fifteen or sixteen, and I still like him. I memorized a lot of him, so I don't even read him now. Yeats. Stevens. Rimbaud. Keats, especially in the odes and the letters. Coleridge, partly. Blake, Shakespeare. I mean, it goes on and on.

Hart Crane?

Hart Crane, certainly. Definitely Hart Crane. And George Oppen, to give you a counterbalance to Crane. Both of them were around at the same time; Oppen is amazing. Totally different from Crane, and we haven't even gone outside the language, I guess, except for Rimbaud. Pavese, Lorca—the list goes on and on once I start mentioning names. Reverdy, whom I translated at one point but whom I finally gave up on. Borges. Vallejo. Neruda. It's impossible: this thing of influence, it changes, you see, day by day. There was a day last winter when I realized how strongly I'd been influenced by Milan Kundera, who I think is wonderful at what he does. I read fiction, too, because good fiction is so vastly sophisticated about language. I like Barth and Hass but I also like Gardner, and his rebuke of the metafictionalists—it's all interesting. Ashbery, of course. So I'm omnivorous, heterodox. I might like to have some sort of clean lineage, but I don't. And it would be silly, anyway, to exclude contradictory influences.

What about painting? A lot of reviewer's of Dollmaker's Ghost *mention your Hopper poem, speak of what they see as your debt to Hopper.*

I like Hopper a lot. When I saw the exhibit in New York with Philip Levine and David St. John, I was impressed. I sympathize with Hopper because he's a guy who, who knew more than he let on somehow. He pretended to be one kind of painter, out of Adrian Henri, whom he later rebuked for all the right reasons. Yet he never took part of in newer currents such as action painting. He was always there, just doing what he did. There's also something poetical about Hopper's paintings. Their characters make me feel like writing the story or the poem *within* the painting. It's a childlike appeal. Nobody knows how to make light work on skin in its utter whiteness the way Hopper does. Utter whiteness is scary: it can be erotic in an incredible way, and one which seems contradictory— eros and terror. I mean, he used to think that light, sunlight, was actually a white and not a yellow. He even said he didn't really want to paint characters, that people were mistaken when they looked at his characters, that what he really wanted to do was paint sunlight on the side of walls. Maybe the real thing, for him, was the unpeopled landscape of paintings such as *Early Sunday Morning*. But I like his people as much or more than his landscapes.

How about music?

Well, I listen to jazz, to Coltrane especially. I really disagree with Larkin. I read an interview with him the other day in *Paris Review* and in it he says that jazz went all wrong with Charlie Parker. I really can't believe that he said that. All the earlier jazz, Bechet, Joplin, et cetera, he considers interrupted and destroyed by Parker. Well, the other thing coming in, it seems to me, was really important: it gave us Parker; Parker gave us Monk, Miles, Coltrane, it was remarkable. And then newer people like Lee Morgan and even Keith Jarrett, whom I like very much although he seems probably a little "pretty" compared to somebody down there like Coltrane, or Miles Davis—a little decorative. I also listen to classical music and rock 'n' roll. I was listening today to Rickie Lee Jones. There are some new people I like: I like X and a band from Hoboken called the Individuals. I like the Clash. I like them but I feel they're becoming . . . oh, I don't know, popular now instead of what they could be. I like the Who, I like Townsend. I've always liked the Rolling Stones. There are other people: Bobby Womack, who goes back. It's odd to talk about them because a reader will think, "Well, that's just rock 'n' roll." Well, that *is* just rock 'n' roll, but the ways in which you can phrase lyrics are very complex, much like phrasing in poetry.

We think of poetry as being such a high art, and it sometimes is, but we also live in this room we share, which is much wider than poetry and includes people like the Jam. A singer can teach you a lot about how a voice is used, and that can influence what you can do in poetry with tone. What I was talking about with caesuras, about slowing and pausing with phrasing—it's akin to what a singer does with phrasing. It's odd: but thinking of rock 'n' roll brings me back to punctuation. The comma still *means* something to me: if the comma's there, it means that you pause. You can't read over it. And hyphens are even stronger, although it's kind of adolescent to use them as much as I do. Really kind of silly. I must look like a high school girl in Oregon writing her first theme. But that's part of phrasing, you see: to stop something and then pick it up again, the movement of mind. And it's musical, it's a musical phrase. Singers, because of the way they have to pause, can show you a lot about doing it gracefully. I mean, when you listen to Billie Holiday or somebody who's a great *pauser,* a great withholder, and then a great giver, it's breathtaking.

What about cinema? I ask specifically because your narratives in your poems develop less like literary narratives than as cinematic narratives—they work with jump cuts, fade-outs, with all sorts of cinematic devices.

Well, that's something we have in poetry, we actually have had it for a long time, mostly because of the nature of the line and the nature of insight commenting upon the imagination. At least it's been true since the Romantics, this shift or "jump cut," if that's what you mean. Film learned it from *poetry.* I don't think you have that in classical poetry; I think Roland Barthes points that out, that all the musculatures in a classical mode are all syntactical: there are none of the abrupt shifts you see in modern poetry, which he says connects a reader to absolutes: childhood, fire, madness, nature.

The classical mode works toward oneness rather than juxtaposition.

It works toward utter coherence. You can think of *The Odyssey* as *the* great alibi for coming home late. The function it serves, at least gauged syntactically, is all dutifully public. I mean, there is no psychoanalysis. When Ulysses is troubled and must decide he says: "In the deep division of my heart it seemed best . . ." Sail on. But going back to film . . . Film's important to me, especially early Fellini films like *La Strada, La Dolce Vita,* and *8½.* And I like the French, Truffaut particularly. Godard's *Breathless.* Bertolucci in *The Conformist* and *Before the Revolution.* All those films said a great deal to me. I thought *The Deer Hunter* was very moving. I felt anxious for days after seeing it, though the second film Cimino did was a disaster. And I've hardly even mentioned American films. I grew up watching them and they were obviously great: Hitchcock, Ford. But I'm not sure how films influence me. I'm not sure how I know how anything influences me at this point. I'm sure that there were very definite influences on me as a child that had to do with my life, whereas the later literary influences let me *see* my life, and this was thanks to the poets I worked with—Philip Levine particularly and Donald Justice and Philip Booth as well. And I was influenced later by friends such as David St. John and Marcia Southwick. She and I wrote very different sorts of poems, but there were always things in her work that influenced me. Bly and Wright were *big* influences, and Plath and Kinnell and Snodgrass and Lowell and Snyder and Larkin and Bishop. And many others.

What was Levine like as a teacher?

Fantastic. Unbelievably sweet and funny and harder than anybody else I've ever seen. But his great talent in teaching was to make you laugh at your own mistakes so that you could overcome them almost cathartically within a few days. Going to a class taught by Philip Levine was like going to no other class on earth. It was going to a class taught by a man who was, for one thing, a master comedian—and also one who had great passion, and who could change the emotion of the class immediately and you could suddenly participate in some dark meditation by Hardy or Yeats on death. He'd read the poem aloud and then would bring it all the way back home to the level of emotion and humor. It wasn't so much going to a class; it wasn't anything *like* a class. It was like going to hear life and poetry and the unbelievable coincidence of the two. It's nothing I've seen anybody else do, and it was particularly important to me when I was between the ages of eighteen and twenty-two, when I studied with Philip. Peter Everwine was also a wonderful poet and a wonderful teacher. Then I went to graduate school and studied with Donald Justice. Justice, unlike Levine, didn't care what you said but cared deeply about the phrasing and your care with saying something. And it was an incredible refinement: you learned so much about *words* studying with Justice; not only words, but also their nuances and their music. You could write *anything* you wanted in his classes: you were unbelievably liberated from any preconception, even those you had about your own work and what *you* wanted to do. He has the most unique mind I've ever met and one of the richest and kindest.

You mentioned David St. John. What other writers of your own generation do you admire?

Anderson. Hass. Marcia Southwick, for sure, because she's so good at what she does. When her work really began to happen, I was there with her, and it was shocking to recognize someone moving from an imagistic and stylized poetry into a poetry of immediate presence and power. She was so sweet: she brought me this poem and said, "How can I make this into a poem?" But it *was* a poem! There were these shocking inner meditations she had that were quite amazing. I learned a lot from her. Carolyn Forché is a friend whom I learn from. Also Michael Burkard, Denis Johnson, Carol Muske. I could go on and on, you know.

You've taught creative writing at several universities and you've edited Missouri Review. *A number of poets one talks to feel that teaching and editing sap some of the same energy that one would usually devote to one's own writing, that ultimately this damages one's potential as a writer. How do you feel about that?*

Oh, God, I feel you can only write poetry for about three hours a day—five at the most when you're really there doing it—and you've got to do something else with the rest of your time. I *like* teaching. I never liked editing, but I do it because *Missouri Review* is there, where I teach. I don't enjoy editing and I'm one of the wariest of editors. Teaching doesn't sap me. I used to work jobs where I'd work in a warehouse or a cannery or drive a truck ten hours a day: *that* saps you. If you work for ten hours a day or eight hours in a physical job or even an office job, I'll tell you one thing: you may have a lot to say, but you won't have any energy to say it. If you don't go to sleep and stay up writing a poem, which is the way I write poems—far into the night—and suddenly it's sunrise and I'm there and maybe I've got a first draft of a poem, and its time to go to sleep for a few hours, that's one life—and not an easy one. But if you have to get up at 5:30 to drive a truck, you won't do that. No one has the stamina to keep doing both things.

Your new manuscript is tentatively titled Trouble. *How do its concerns and method differ from* Dollmaker's Ghost?

Well, for one thing, there are no personas being used: there's no ghost network going on. An odd thing happened to me one day in New York. Marcia and I were staying with an old friend of ours and we'd all gone out the night before. Stephen Dunn had had dinner with us and come over briefly for a drink. It was great to see him—he's an old, old friend— we'd talked and drunk a lot of scotch during the night. The next day I got up; and it was a beautiful day in New York; I went around the corner to get bagels to bring back for breakfast, and I had this sudden idea of myself being able to say something that was terribly frank and honest and uncompromising and which might, in fact, be poetry. I was thinking that it was *poetry* and that it was what I really wanted to do, to say something terribly unequivocal. Not a literal or pedestrian honesty but an honesty of the imagination. And I've thought a lot about that moment—it disappeared, it evaporated almost immediately after coming back in and having coffee and bagels and cream cheese and all that and talking about nothing, talking about the *New York Times,* talking about this and that, listening to whoever was on the radio. But I'll never forget that moment: it was an avenue into something, and it made me understand what I really wished to do in my poetry. In my life. I understood the kind of power I've always wanted to have in poetry. It is a sort of energy, the way Yeats has it in, say, "Easter 1916," when his energy isolates a moment in time and makes it stay there forever and live in that present. It's what Eliot means when he talks about that Chinese vase, with its pattern always moving, and yet always still. And I think I felt that I could have that quality by talking very *directly* in a poem. That's what I'm doing now—just talking very directly from a first-person viewpoint during a rocky time in my own life. My father died about a year ago; my wife and I separated in August; we have a son. . . . All these things coalesced at one point. I used to think that one could only write about such things long after they had happened. But it seemed to me that there was no other choice but to try to write about them *as* they happened. Now maybe this is wrong. But there seemed to be nothing else to say, to talk about. . . . Anyway, that's what the book seems to be about. I didn't plan it that way. I didn't imagine that I even could write directly about things that had just happened; but I finally discovered that if I tried to stay off subjects like that, I felt foolish. I don't want to be a "professional" and just write competent poems. I'd rather go into the whole sorrow of the beast, or whatever the phrase is, and try to talk about it. I may fail, but that's all right.

What makes a major poet?

Who knows? Time. Complexity. Character, probably. I don't hold character up as being The Great Thing, by the way. It's a vital mask over the consistency or persistency of neuroses or madness, of being floored by being. That's what character is, a vast defense mechanism. It's nothing to be terribly proud of, though we say it is, espouse it in our culture. And it is, of course: it's heroic in a social circumstance. But if you're ever confronted by someone who has no defenses—who is *beyond* character, who is certainly beyond caring about that, who's totally human and who asks you something so honest, probably the most honest question you've heard in your life—that's something else. What I'm talking about is finding a way to combine the two things, to have character (you can't get *away* from your own, anyway) and to ask something with the unbelievable honesty of a man who is about to vanish from the world. That was the vision I had in New York. We're so proud sometimes of things that keep us from the utter phenomenon of being alive—because it is frightening to realize that you are alive, that you *are* at all.

You're thirty-six, and Stevens, Yeats, Williams, a number of the major poets of this century really didn't start writing in what I guess you'd say is a "grand manner" until they were in their sixties. What would you like your achievement to be like thirty years from now?

I don't know. I can't really say. I would like to write my poems and leave it at that. I used to envy other poets. I'd read Bidart and say, "I wish I had his way of not being 'poetic' at all and yet being incredibly talented." I love his work. Or I envied the eroticism of David St. John's poems, which is ingrained so deeply in his language—there's a desire his *words* have for each other. But now I just want to write my own poems. I would like to be one of those people who was, in poetry, a rule breaker; someone who mattered. Poetry sometimes seems totally enclosed or secluded world, a very tiny one: everybody knows what everybody else is going through by virtue of this incredible grapevine, so much so that the other worlds are closed off to us. I think poetry ought to challenge these other worlds in the way that fiction can challenge science or that art can challenge technology. I don't know how to do that in an exciting way in poetry, and I don't want her to disappear into a mist of jargon in the process. I wouldn't want to put her in conditions where she couldn't even breathe. Poetry's such an ancient art—we still have a belief in the muse. Can you imagine any other art or any other way of thinking that still has something like *that*? You know, it's so old, and the intimacy you feel with other poets is so revealing and right—it's like no other thing that anyone else on earth has. I respect poetry, because it's very old and yet it's also new and renewing. When I think of myself thirty years from now, I have this trepidation about saying *anything*. I don't *know* what will happen; I don't know who will be around to read me, or whether I'm a shriek in the void. But it is obvious that some works might last—I do feel that.

One of the things Wallace Stevens said: "No one understands that one writes poetry because one must."

Yeah, must. Also, it's just better than living any other way. I mean, *I* think it's better. I still think poetry is healthy; it also has greater purity than anything else, if only because you can use the mind all the way up. You can exist in the liberated adulthood of poetry, totally uncompromised.

So That: On Holub's "Meeting Ezra Pound"

Time is a violation, someone once remarked in a lecture hall, and then went on to say that the time in which one is born is a violation, that time itself is a violation committed against everyone alive. It makes us finite, and therefore the violation is always personal: its final form is both banal and intimate, for it is simply one's death, but finally all of us get the idea, an idea which is actually the absence of any idea and, therefore, unimaginable. About as close as one can get to a statement of it is: "The meaning of life is that it stops." And there it is: the empty, white, blank, unblinking center of it all.

It was an elaborately lovely way of saying the most obvious thing of all, and the pleasure was in the elaboration, and that, I think now, was the whole point of doing it, saying it there, in the first place, the pleasure of reformulating it. . . .

Meeting Ezra Pound

I don't know what came first, poets or festivals.

Nevertheless, it was a festival that caused me to meet Ezra Pound.

They seated him in a chair on a square in Spoleto and pushed me towards him. He took the hand I extended and looked with those light blue eyes right through my head, way

---

This translation of Holub's poem by Dana Hábová and Stuart Friebert appeared in conjunction with this essay in *Field* 49 (fall 1993): 12–17.

off into the distance. That was all. He didn't move after that. He didn't let go of my hand, he forgot the eyes. It was a lasting grip, like a gesture of a statue. His hand was icy and stony. It was impossible to get away.

I said something. The sparrows chirruped. A spider was crawling on the wall, tasting the stone with its forelegs. A spider understanding the language of a stone.

A freight was passing through the tunnel of my head. A flagman in blue overalls waved gloomily from the last car.

It is interesting how long it takes for a freight train like that to pass by.

Then they parted us.

My hand was cold too, as if touching the Milky Way.

So that a freight train without a schedule exists. So that a spider on a stone exists. So that a hand alone and a hand per se exists. So that a meeting without meeting exists and a person without a person. So that a tunnel exists—a whole network of tunnels, empty and dark, interconnecting the living matter which is called poetry at festivals.

So that I may have met Ezra Pound, only I sort of did not exist in that moment.[1]

Holub's poem is, among other things, an elegy, and maybe my remembrance of that voice in that lecture hall isn't inappropriate, especially because one theme Pound introduces and repeats in his *Cantos* is this one: "Time is the evil." And Holub, if we attend to the precision of what is supposedly a vague phrase, and isn't, concurs: "only I sort of did not exist in that moment." For "sort of" is precise, at least in the American idiom of the translation. It means that condition common to all of us, just beneath all possible explanation of *that* "moment," *that* violation.

But what first fascinated me about Holub's poem had nothing to do with any of this. What I first noticed was a little riff, an echo, a variation, or so I thought. But it wasn't an echo nor any real variation. It was repetition. It was two notes from someone else's music, the two notes repeated no less than *six* times toward the close of Holub's prose poem. As if in answer to something. But to what? To this, I think:

Cypri munimenta sortita est, mirthful, orichalchi, with
　　golden
Girdles and breast bands, thou with dark eyelids
Bearing the golden bough of Argicida. So that:
　　　　　　　　　　　　　　—Ezra Pound, Canto 1

So that what? I still wonder. In Pound's odd finale to his open-
ing *Canto,* those two notes, that spondee, are not closure at all.
The phrase leaves us looking off into space, at the cliff's edge,
with only a colon as a guardrail. Pound violates, as in fact he
has already interrupted, his translation of book 11 of *The Odys-
sey* from a Renaissance Latin source, itself a translation, so
that . . . But that's just the trouble with it. "So that:" is just *left*
there, staving off closure on the way to Hell so that everything
might continue. . . .

But does every poet go to Hell, just because Homer, Virgil,
Dante, Milton, and Pound have? Is Holub going there? Or is
that just Holub's problem, and, in a way, our own, that it isn't
possible for us to get there anymore, that Hell has become the
sound of chalk screeching on a blackboard in an auditorium,
someone else's paradigm, bundle of connections, history's
abandoned spiderweb with its cockeyed embroidery you can
look right through? Look through to what?

The riptides and gnarly surf that *The Cantos* are so famous for,
all the discontinuities of the polyvocal, spatial, juxtaposed,
referential form, conceal the larger quest of the poem, which
is passionately involved in a dream of *continuity,* not its oppo-
site. And critical terms, like those above, try to protect us from
a poem that is, therefore, passionately involved in its own
failure. Pound said of it, at the end, "It won't . . . cohere" and
"I botched it." And certainly what moves us in *The Pisan Cantos*
is the poet's awareness of just how wrong he has been, what
moves us is how the poet endures the tragedy of his name.

Holub arrives at the scene, intent here on restoring what con-
tinuity he can to the meeting, and yet ends up in a place at once
too similar to Pound's, and too different, a place that becomes
space: "So that I may have met . . ."

So that. If we take the occasion of the poem seriously, it's
impossible not to hear that insistent repetition as anything less
than an answer, even though it is an answer that fails.

OK, so what happens? Holub takes Pound's hand. But then Pound won't let go of his hand. Or isn't able to let go of it. Or forgets to. Pretty soon Holub is holding hands, not with Pound, not with anyone, but with space itself, which has a surprisingly tight, light grip.

"How is it far if I think it?" was the question Pound asked in *The Cantos*. For Pound, for the modernists generally, it was never far. But in this curious scene, Holub is by now holding hands with the Milky Way. Pound is dying and his death is inevitable. He is alive and he is not alive and Holub is with him and not with him in this moment.

Holub brilliantly avoids the kitsch of a delusional *ars poetica* here, for it might be consoling to think that "living matter" is, categorically, poetry. But Holub is too tough for a kind of thinking which overrates all things. His qualification is searing: "the living matter which is called poetry at festivals."

At festivals.

One need only to compare a literary festival with an ancient one to note, with Holub and Pound, what has been lost, or what we all assume has been lost. After all, we have little way of knowing what those festivals were like, and so we invest them with a vanished reality. Who knows? Maybe the dancers on Crete were bored out of their minds like adolescents in a catechism class. Since we can never know, we speculate, we "invest" in the ancient ritual, and invest it with significance. How could we do otherwise?

World War II destroyed the modernists' paradigms, their systems, mythical methods, their luxuriant organic forms. Time is a violation. "It's a faster game now, and a ruder one," said Ransom at the dawn of our era. If one wants to see the difference in sharp relief, he should listen to first lines on tapes Harvard has produced, first to Wallace Stevens: "This is where the serpent lives, the bodiless"; and then to John Berryman: "Life, friends, is boring." The idiom travels a long way between the two.

What typifies the era, the one we live in now?

For Pound, it was never far if he could think it. For us, what is near is often far away from us, what is far off remains remote even when we erase the distance between it and us,

Heidegger thought. Heidegger thought our anxiety about the atom bomb was strange considering that "the terrible has already happened." It isn't that we can't get "there" from here; we can. What is terrible is that we simply can no longer get *here* from there.

And this I think is why Holub and his translators, who are brilliantly comic, absent, and relentless in this elegy, have chosen to represent the age in all its paucity, its frailty, the neutral modesty and honesty of the concluding figure in which "sort of" is given its full range at last, the idiom reminding me of those in wet suits, surfing off Capitola, spinning out just as the gray wall of rock looms up suddenly in front of them.

"Sort of" isn't glory. "Sort of" isn't tragedy. And that is the point. That is also the trouble. Holub's imagination, which does typify our time, seems to move at the speed of light. It delivers us from history, so that in this way, Holub's elegy becomes a kind of birth. Everything comes rushing back into his poem but it's all without history: a train, a tunnel, a hand per se and a hand alone. And even though it is a birth in a world that is now a vast orphanage, there's something familiar about it, "homey" even, for it's *our* vast orphanage. What would we do without it, and the irony of its ceaseless catcalls and whistles? I like to think that the poet who will write its epitaph is three hours old at this moment, only I sort of doubt it.

Some Notes on Grief and the Image

My grief is that I bear no grief
& so I bear myself. I know I live apart.
—Jon Anderson

The ocean comes to grieving men.
—Robert Bly

Although it must be living itself that leads anyone to *conditions of grief,* it may be a poet's obsession with the Image that leads to grieving. But how so? Why? If an image is, as Pound said, "an intellectual and emotional complex in an instant of time," it is exactly that "instant of time" which passes; even though an image may reify itself many times in a reader's experience, it will pass again as well. The image draws on, comes out of, the "world of the senses" and, therefore, originates in a world that passes, that is passing, every moment. Could it be, then, that every image, *as image,* has this quality of poignancy and vulnerability since it occurs, and occurs so wholeheartedly, in time?

Pound's definition above gives us a limited, if nearly adequate, idea of the image. So we have known for years that the Image is not a photograph, that it engages or can engage any of the senses, and, if we want to illustrate this, we can remember the tactile imagery of Keats in "Eve of St. Agnes" or the imagery of sound in Roethke's *North American Sequence,* or, in Whitman, all of the senses. But why, both in the popular imagination and among poets, is there this persistent fault in the way we think of the Image? Usually, people think of and remember images as if

From *Of Solitude and Silence: Writings on Robert Bly,* ed. Kate Daniels and Richard Jones (Boston: Beacon Press, 1981), 170–75.

nearly all of them were *seen*. And why are so many images composed, and I would include much of the use of the Deep Image, for the eye itself? "Old warships drowning in a raindrop" is a visual image before it is in any way a conceptual one. I would suggest that much of our use of imagery in contemporary poetry is related to the eye, to sight, more often than to smell, taste, touch, or hearing. Perhaps eyesight is the most developed sense that we have, and perhaps the very activities of reading and writing engage, too wholly, the eye. I think the problem, if it *is* a problem, may be cultural as well, however. None of us can really escape our culture, and our culture conditions us through the use of film and photography almost daily. And photographs, whether on the front page of the *New York Times* or in museums, are, *literally,* time that has been made to hold still. As such, they remind us, because they are images unmediated by language, of time itself. Perhaps, as Roland Barthes indicates in *Camera Lucida,* each photograph, but especially portraits and landscapes, are, in the "realism," slight deaths, slight catches in the breath, too, especially if they are intellectually and emotionally complex. And yet I do not mean to suggest that photography is limited to a kind of literal representationality, a total realism of the eye. The work of Minor White and Aaron Siskind disproves this, and many of their prints resemble not what the eye sees, but what it didn't then see, at the moment when the shutter clicked. In the darkroom, after the eye has done its other work, the photograph grows into something more like a Franz Kline canvas, and less and less like a factory or a river bed. And all that is, by now, an old story: some photographers wish to go beyond the camera; some painters wish to go beyond paint; some poets wish to go beyond words. Some go beyond and do not come back. Many live and work in two worlds which are like unidentical twins. The pleasure is in the tension.

That image, "Old warships drowning in a raindrop" goes beyond the natural phenomena observable to the eye, and yet stays within the boundaries of what can be seen but never is really seen in experience. We call such an image surrealistic. But it is only partly so. The image never totally severs its connection to the eye; therefore, to realism, to *imagined* phenomena.

To go *beyond* in any final sense is to go mute in a final sense. One of the purest surrealist acts, it was said, was to blindfold yourself and to walk to a busy street corner, turn around a few times, and then to fire a pistol into the crowd. Why the blindfold? So you would not see. This makes, of course, the shooting more fair and more disinterested. You could kill a prince or a *plongeur* with equal ease and abandon. But more importantly, the blindfold kills already, inwardly, the realist inside yourself so that the other person can be released, that "other" who fires the pistol, the one who has already left this world. The trouble with words is that they are in and out of the world. They want to be specific. They want to *mean*, even if we no longer quite want them to mean in the ways they wish to mean. Once, I was talking to a friend over lunch. He had studied in Switzerland, and I wanted to ask him about Saussure, about *sign* and *signifier* and *signified.* Our talk eddied out, as I had hoped it would because I wanted to learn something about contemporary criticism. I finally asked him if he thought that anything held the word, or the signifier, to the thing, or the signified. His answer was simple. "Yes," he said, "desire."

Perhaps the Image, like a thing or an animal or a human, desires to be, to be itself eternally. The Image is like us, but it is not like us. It desires to constellate itself beyond us, and to live apart from us. It may or may not desire to fit into the fabric of the whole work of art, to be "organic" in *that* shopworn sense of the word. In truth, *we* pass, and the Image becomes more moving to us because it remains and at the same time records something that passes. The images we write hold still, and their stillness is curious because it reminds us that, someday, up ahead, at the end of the story, completion is inevitable but comprehensible. Freud called it "the riddle of death," but a riddle is also an image, a stillness.

A Ramage for the Star Man, Mourning

The star man, mourning, floats among the stars
firmly, the farms beneath his feet.
How long it takes to climb into grief!
Fifty years old, and still held in the dark,

in the unfinished, the hopeful, what longs for
solution.
As that girl there, who explains things, combing
her hair . . . the face seems alert, the body
still drifting through the ponderous farms of
ocean.

In some of Robert Bly's most recent work, the condition of grief
and mourning is what the poet hopes to accomplish. Bly longs
to be taken into something, constellated and completed. He
desires to "climb into grief," and his image of it here is an
attempt to define its condition, a condition beyond time, and
beyond the merely "hopeful." Why beyond the merely hope-
ful? When we witness the harrowing completeness of tragedy,
we rarely think that such art is "positive" or "negative" in its
final effect, since tragedy is in some way a machine designed to
purge us and to devour these two poles, the "positive" and the
"negative," these two illusions. It is designed to make us "grow
up." I suppose that people who truly desire only "something
uplifting" in art are adolescents. People who want only their
own cynicism confirmed by art are also, probably, adolescents.
But Bly's little poem is no tragedy, and toward its end, Bly's
method becomes uncharacteristically modest and renuncia-
tory. An unidentified girl, combing her hair, is explaining
things. We are not told what these are. The final line of the
poem introduces evolution, myth, and the line bores me, as
does the opening of the poem. Yet I am drawn to the human
statements, the renunciatory tone taken in the midst of the
poem, its declaration, made barrenly and without any image, of
the desire for a condition of grief. And that girl, combing her
hair, so like the poet and yet so unlike him, is the true mirror of
the poem. It seems to me, then, that the ocean she is still drift-
ing through does not complete the poem. Nothing completes
the poem. It is, for now, unfinished. And that is what Bly al-
ready realizes in the poem. Completeness is the condition he
longs for, and the "ocean" simply muddies the experience with
its image, which is complete only in itself and which has little to
do with the poem. But the man behind that image, like the
Wizard of Oz behind his great machine, or like Robert Bly

behind his masks at a poetry reading, is admitting here that he is, after all, only a man, and fifty, and "unfinished."

But at least Bly has set out here on another journey, and, as he has written elsewhere, "The ocean comes to grieving men." There is only one problem with men who grieve absolutely. They may be beyond language, or language may no longer have any real hold on them. In Fellini's *La Strada,* the circus performer and strong man, Zampano the Great, murders accidentally and out of passion, and therefore is left totally alone, and so in the last scene crawls on his knees to the sea. That is a condition of grief. There may be other conditions, but they are no longer Zampano's. The problem for a lyric poet is that he cannot grieve, in words, for himself. The artist in that last scene is, after all, not Zampano, but Fellini. The conditions of actual grief may not permit the poet to speak.

Mock Mockers after That

Mock mockers after that
That would not lift a hand maybe
To help good, wise or great.
—"Nineteen Hundred and Nineteen"

My epigraph from Yeats has to do with elegies. But before I begin my discussion, I want to suggest that this is not just a critical matter, mostly because I am not a critic, it is a personal one. I wrote an elegy once for a friend of mine, a friend from high school who died in Vietnam. When it has been praised, I have always felt that there was a curious injustice at work. My friend Eddie Zamora grew up where I did in central California and dropped out of junior college, therefore lost his 2S deferment by dropping out, therefore was drafted, therefore died in Vietnam. He was Chicano–Mexican American—I was Anglo. Because my circumstances were more comfortable and because my parents could afford to keep me in college, I had a 2S deferment. It was that kind of privilege that allowed me to live and allowed my friend to die, but my poem is praised. What I am reminded of when that occurs is the considerable injustice in circumstances that allowed that to happen. There is also, quite simply, the guilt of surviving. So-and-so is dead and you are alive.

Although they are not tricks, elegies are tricky things. In the study of the form in English, the poet and critic Peter Sacks suggests that not all poets escape from elegies they write without attendant feelings of guilt, anxiety, and the sense of

This essay was delivered as a lecture at the Warren Wilson MFA Seminar for Writers in Swannanoa, North Carolina, in January 1994. This version, edited by Ruth Anderson Barnett, is reprinted from the *Marlboro Review* (winter–spring 1997): 61–73.

some further obligation that comes upon them surprisingly, either within the wake of what they have written or within the elegy itself. For such feelings of guilt, anxiety, and obligation are what they have created as well, are the sometimes unforeseen by-products of the elegiac act, while the elegy itself becomes, of course, public, social, part of a culture which defines not only the conventions of the elegy, but also what the work of mourning and consolation is. Insofar as elegies are also this work of mourning and consolation, they serve two significantly opposed, contradictory functions. For if they commemorate and remember the dead, they also inter the dead, bury them; and, in closing, the poet, Sacks says, seeks a new object for his affection elsewhere, as in "fresh woods, and pastures new."

In short, the poet betrays the figure of the beloved or respected, even as he memorializes it; "thus the source of love turns into the object of love," Joseph Brodsky concludes in his elegy for Auden. And what is apparent there is that the elegiac act has changed the one it was written for, has made, of what had been so recently human, a representation.

This problem, or predicament, this entire presumption of writing for the dead, presents some poets with an ethical unease, similar to that of lyrical confessional poets who, for better or worse, seem capable of writing only of the self. But after all, betrayal is betrayal, even if it is only self-betrayal. (Or, as Adrienne Rich once phrased it, "what sort of beast would turn itself into words?") But the violation that occurs in the elegiac act is sometimes more serious. If the so-called confessional poet feels dismay, embarrassment, sometimes shame in showing off his scars in print, he at least harms no one but himself. The elegy always involves another, and the poet, working in his elegy toward what he expects to be catharsis and release, sometimes finds them only at the cost of being accused and reprimanded by the being whom he has turned into a figure, into a literary convention which, by its own definition, has little alternative but to falsify the life and death it preys upon. "Little alternative" because it exists in words and because, as we are by now tired of hearing, words transform experience more than they record it.

Sacks makes a compelling argument in his study that this guilt, anxiety, and obligation are Oedipal in origin and this may be so if one follows one's feelings to their source and if one is equipped with the proper road map to the symbolic order, that is, the one first provided by Freud and then updated by Lacan. But isn't the dilemma simpler? Aren't the guilt and anxiety a poet or anyone else experiences more akin to the remorse or guilt of the survivor? After all, the poet lives. The beloved other does not. As one of the dead friends who surfaces in Seamus Heaney's Dantesque pilgrimage in *Station Island* puts it:

> I felt that I should have seen far more of you
> and maybe would have—but dead at thirty-two!
> Ah poet, lucky poet, tell me why
> what seemed deserved and promised passed me by?

Remorse and not guilt may be the appropriate term for the regret one feels when one has done something wrong, and I wonder if it isn't the term here? For the sin of the survivor, poet or not, sometimes consists simply in still being alive at all. The poet's sin is compounded by the very act of writing an elegy. If elegies exist primarily as a way of completing the processes of grief, mourning, and consolation, they are then involved in processes all people have in common, processes that are private.

What are the larger implications of writing, then of publishing such processes? Who are elegies really for and why? W. S. Merwin, in the following poem, aspires, on the surface at least, to a state of altruistic brevity. It simply goes like this:

Elegy

Who would I show it to?

But the very fact that the thing exists, that we read it, undermines the sentiment.

Carried to extremes, of course, all these ethical scruples become ridiculous. If elegies are so morally wrong in the first place, what should one do? Forget the dead? Leave no written memorial to their existence? Is ignoring them ethically better than writing about them? If so, while we are doing this, we can probably forget history in its entirety. It just isn't an either/or question. Poetry may be a bit more enlightening than theory on all this. As Jon Anderson writes at the end of his poem "Creative Writing," as a kind of farewell address to students,

> I don't want to trouble you; you are entering history.
> . . . .
> after death there are two alternatives,
> both heartless:
> memory & forgetfulness.

Memory recalls the dead without regard for the misery such reminders may cause us, and only by a deliberately heartless act may we forget them.

Finally, I would ask whether such moral scrupulousness in regard to the elegy is even possible. If elegies turn lives into representations, well, what, in reality, does our ordinary daily consciousness do? Don't others we know, even those we know intimately, conform in one way or another to that representation of them that we make daily and cannot help making, however biased or inaccurate or idealized it may be? Why else would feminists justifiably complain and react against what they term a masculine essentializing of women? If elegies are so obviously not really, not entirely written for the dead, in what sense then is the work of mourning public rather than private and the experience worldly and held in common with the culture around it?

Sacks writes the following: "At the most obvious level, we recall Freud's suggestion that the superego is made up of the 'illustrious dead,' a sort of cultural reservoir, or rather cemetery, in which one may also inter one's renounced love-objects and in which the ruling monument is the internalized figure of the father." I note the shocking wording of this phrase—"inter ones renounced love objects"—because I think it accurately describes Sacks's theory of the paradoxical intentions of the elegy itself. If the theory is persuasive, I suppose it is primarily because one recognizes the presence of what Freud called the superego through its symptoms. What are its symptoms? Guilt, anxiety, the sense of a further task or obligation—that is what the superego would be for most people. (If you were born as I was, raised as a Catholic by an Irish mother, the situation is, of course, different because in that system to have been born at all is, to some extent, politically incorrect.)

Well, if these feelings of guilt, and so forth, remain wholly internal and private, they don't have much effect in terms of poetry, but what has an effect in life usually has an effect on art as well. The clearest, most abundant, recent example of how this guilt, anxiety, and obligation function after an elegy has been written occurs in the work of Seamus Heaney, where the existence of an earlier elegiac poem, "The Strand at Lough Beg," causes a visionary meeting between Heaney and his slain cousin, Colum McCartney, in section 8 of *Station Island*.

It is interesting that the dead, who often inhabit Heaney's elegies, are not just dead; they are more often victims like McCartney, a victim of factional political assassination, or are accidental, nonpartisan victims of political violence, like the fisherman in "Casualty." Their presence is striking in a poet who for years had been criticized for avoiding direct confrontation, in his work at least, with what have been called the "troubles" in Northern Ireland. In fact, the strongest criticism mounted against Heaney accused him not of political neutrality, a state of grace which even the poet admits would be impossible, but of an indifference akin to the aesthetic sensibility of the modernist artist, the kind of attitude relevant to this discussion that one notes in Joyce's characterization of his own book, *Dubliners*. To quote, "I wrote it in a style of scrupulous meanness." Yet Heaney's recognition of the conflict in Ulster, his inclusion of it in a poetry that chronicles the history of violence and injustice in his native land, that takes note of those young women "cauled in tar" on bridge railings as punishment for their involvement with British soldiers occupying Belfast ("Punishment"), is of crucial importance to his achievement and growth as a poet. It is a difficult thing to do because, on the one hand, the poet must engage a violent political dilemma without ignoring his own membership in it. On the other, he has to write poetry, not propaganda.

But the question Heaney addressed at Station Island is far more troubling. What if the dead, including the already elegized dead, won't stay dead? Heaney concludes "The Strand at Lough Beg" in the following rather elegiacally conventional manner:

Across that strand of yours the cattle graze
Up to their bellies in an early mist
And now they turn their unbewildered gaze
To where we work our way through squeaking sedge
Drowning in dew. Like a dull blade with its edge
Honed bright, Lough Beg half shines under the haze.
I turn because the sweeping of your feet
Has stopped behind me, to find you on your knees
With blood and roadside muck in your hair and eyes,
Then kneel in front of you in brimming grass
And gather up cold handfuls of the dew
To wash you, cousin. I dab you clean with moss
Fine as the drizzle out of a low cloud.
I lift you under the arms and lay you flat.
With rushes that shoot green again, I plait
Green scapulars to wear over your shroud.

The figuration that concludes this elegy, its abundant pastoral imagery, the elegiac action of cleansing the dead with vegetation of some kind, is as ancient, or as old, as the elegy itself. But that blood and roadside muck in the young cousin's hair and eyes is wiped away, I think, too easily. It is wiped away, not by any convincing human action, but by the conventions of the elegy form itself. Therefore, the dead won't stay dead. In section 8 of *Station Island,* the cousin, Colum McCartney, returns, reappears on Heaney's pilgrimage with a bitter family score to settle. Heaney has just been speaking with the shade of his "archaeologist," Tom, who has called Heaney "poet, lucky poet" in the lines quoted earlier. The section continues like this:

I could not speak. I saw a hoard of black
basalt axe handles, smooth as a beetle's back,
a cairn of stone force that might detonate
the eggs of danger. And then I saw a face
he had once given me, a plaster cast
of an abbess, done by the Gowran master,
mild-mouthed and cowled, a character of grace.
"Your gift will be a candle in our house."
But he had gone . . .

And now—notice how quickly—follows a Dantesque passage that gives a sense of the kind of thing Heaney is able to do.

Notice the immediacy, the kind of hallucinatory phantasmagoria that goes on in Dante and in Heaney too as the cousin appears:

> But he had gone, when I looked to meet his eyes
> and hunkering instead there in his place
> was a bleeding, pale-faced boy, plastered in mud.
> "The red hot pokers blazed a lovely red
> in Jerpoint the Sunday I was murdered,"
> he said quietly. "Now do you remember?
> You were there with poets when you got the word
> and stayed there with them, while your own flesh and blood
> was carted to Bellaghy from the Fews.
> They showed more agitation at the news
> than you did."

Now Heaney speaks:

> "But they were getting crisis
> first hand, Colum, they had happened in on
> live sectarian assassination.
> I was dumb, encountering what was destined."
> And so I pleaded with my second cousin.
> "I kept seeing a grey stretch of Lough Beg
> and the strand empty at daybreak.
> I felt like the bottom of a dried-up lake."

The cousin's response:

> "You saw that, and you wrote that—not the fact.
> You confused evasion and artistic tact.
> The Protestant who shot me through the head
> I accuse directly but indirectly, you
> who now atone perhaps upon this bed
> for the way you white-washed ugliness and drew
> the lovely blinds of the *Purgatorio*
> and saccharined my death with morning dew."
> Then I seemed to waken out of steep
> among more pilgrims whom I did not know
> drifting to the hostel for the night.

In his essay, "The Recantation of Beauty," Barry Goldensohn argues, concerning the reappearance of the dead cousin:

"It would be hard to devise a more fundamental denunciation of the politics and morality of "The Strand at Lough Beg." He continues to say that this episode of *Station Island* is a sort of moral center for the whole poem: "Heaney is not fulminating, not accusing himself of lying or propagandizing or comforting the enemy, nor grandly consoling himself for being merely human" (although this last is maybe arguable). "The move," Goldensohn tells us, "is towards locating where the real moral danger lies: namely in that priestly posture that poets take on, dispensing grace and beauty when a colder and clearer vision is called for." This is a sensitive assessment, but something else is happening besides a moral lesson here. Something prior to the origins of ethics, something ancient in the culture and ancient in the psyche. For why else would the slain cousin admit that the poet, in the supposed dream fiction of *Station Island,* atones for anything here? What happens is a mutual kind of witnessing. The cousin, at the moment of his own death, sees Heaney at a gathering of poets, and Heaney, at least from the cousin's account, is able to see the cousin in the agony of his end. In this moment, using only a few details to accompany the scene—tellingly, "the red hot pokers blazed a lovely red"—the cousin's voice, its anger, conveys the injustice of his death. And so, in this moment, Heaney must undergo it in imagination with him. In doing so, he atones, or "perhaps" atones, for atonement in the sense used here is never assured. This is the ritual descent, larger than any moral lesson that Heaney is required to make, and it is the penance beyond prayer that he is required to write out in addition, scribed to the dead cousin he had once betrayed, both in art and in life. In all, the episode is a leveling, humbling experience revealing the exact Dantesque limitation of art by life. In a larger sense, such empathy is simply the necessary recognition that others, alive or dead, are real. Part of a procedure of grief and mourning, inside and outside art, by which a certain grace, atonement and liberation from guilt and anxiety are made possible.

The elegist, if his art is to be authentic, must also die, imaginatively at least, with his subject. But if, after section 8 of *Station Island,* Heaney has atoned for his earlier elegy and for the entire arrogance of the artist in relation to the life around him, what are we to make of the end of this poem? For in section 12, Heaney encounters a literary father figure, James Joyce, and Joyce's appearance here and his message are as troubling as they are liberating:

> "Your obligation
> is not discharged by any common rite.
> What you must do must be done on your own
>
> so get back in harness. The main thing is to write
> for the joy of it. Cultivate a work-lust
> that imagines its haven like your hands at night
> dreaming the sun in the sunspot of a breast.
> You are fasted now, light-headed, dangerous.
> Take off from here. And don't be so earnest,
>
> let others wear the sackcloth and the ashes.
> Let go, let fly, forget.
> You've listened long enough. Now strike your note."
>
> It was as if I had stepped free into space
> alone with nothing that I had not known already.
> Raindrops blew in my face
>
> as I came to.

But the shade of Joyce continues, jeering:

> The English language
> belongs to us. You are raking at dead fires,
>
> waste of time for somebody your age.
> That subject people stuff is a cod's game,
> infantile, like your peasant pilgrimage.
>
> You lose more of yourself than you redeem
> doing the decent thing. Keep at a tangent.
> When they make the circle wide. It's time to swim
>
> out on your own and fill the element
> with signatures on your own frequency;
> echo soundings, searches, probes, allurements,
>
> Elver-gleams in the dark of the whole sea.

The presence of James Joyce here is compelling and seductive. (It is like listening to the pleasure principle itself, if it had a voice, for poets anyway.) But the trouble is that Joyce here remains so much a literary ghost handing out writerly advice that, however subtly and splendidly contrived, this voice feels false to the dramatic structure of the whole poem. It acts merely as a way to escape the poem rather than to end it. It is Joyce's appearance here that causes James Simmons, in "The Trouble with Seamus," to qualify his praise for the good poems in *Station Island* and for its ambitious conception. Simmons believes that the poet is not "wise or clever enough" to warrant "great ghosts from the past" advising him. The idea, Simmons says, is "vain and comic."

Well, I, for one, am just as glad that Heaney is not wise or clever here or elsewhere—although I think he is wise sometimes—for I think there are enough wise and clever poets around nowadays. But I would agree with Simmons's assessment that the ghostly literary figure here presented is vain and comic. Vain because the advice of Joyce lacks in its placement here at the end of a serious and lengthy poem enough contextualization, enough tone, to establish a kind of legibility. As readers, we don't know how to read this last section. We don't know whether we are meant to take Joyce's advice seriously. We aren't even sure that Heaney himself knows how to read that voice, knows whether to take that advice simply on the authority of the patriarchal master. If we do take it seriously, we are left only with the arrogant indifference of a modernist sensibility—one that lacks the ethical commitment that Joyce's work, in fact, had. (That is, no matter how literary his reworking of the Ulysses myth is, what we remember about Joyce are these unforgettable characters, the abundantly present Molly Bloom and the invisible Michael Fury, upon whose passions fate depends.) But Joyce's advice at the end of *Station Island,* despite its political jab at England, is mostly literary advice. By telling Heaney to forget the troubles in Northern Ireland, aren't the reappearance of Colum McCartney, all of section 8, and certain other episodes that are extraordinarily powerful, aren't they all, to some extent mocked? Aren't they made to seem unimportant, in contrast to this final theme of the artist's immortal destiny? In this way the lives and deaths of others become merely mortal, insubstantial, forgettable. But isn't that Joyce's advice? Forget them? Only, if in some way Heaney's presentation, his representation of Joyce were an implicit renunciation on the poet's part of the advice Joyce gives him, could this concluding episode be moving and adequate to the questions the poem has already asked; in other words, if we heard Joyce and Heaney, and we then had the sense that Heaney would like to do what Joyce suggests, but Heaney's own location, in a political context, makes that impossible.

As it is, the advice given, looked at twice, seems selfish and impossible, given the contemporary context of Heaney's Ulster. It is even more unfortunate that this end reminds us that the entire poem is a kind of contraption using Dante's form and acquiescing, if conclusions matter dramatically, and they do, to some Joycean aesthetic. The poem ultimately reinforces his literary influences' artistic authority, not Heaney's, and Heaney is in some measure disgraced and diminished by this as an artist. The ending here is a large structural mistake akin to the kind of belatedly written last ten chapters of *Huckleberry Finn*, when Tom Sawyer appears in the novel and mocks the serious theme Twain has established there, namely that love and freedom are incompatible. And it is no good insisting any more in response to this that poetry has always been literary. Of course it has. Dante needs Virgil in order to know Hell at all. But on the collective behalf of poets, it is clear that Hell is not populated entirely by poets. From Paulo and Francesca to Ciacco, to Ugolino, we are shown an extraordinary panorama of life, a variety. Nor am I criticizing the presence of the literary in poetry. When Philip Levine writes of Lorca or Thomas Lux writes of Keats, there are crucial matters of human concern involved. The heart is at stake in such poems and the heart is not a paper one.

Bear in mind that I am saying all of this within the context of a genuine admiration for Heaney, offering it perhaps as a warning to him and to that generation of poets, now writing in their maturity, who seem at times to be writing under the influence of a heady literary criticism, at times to be writing almost for the literary critic. Heaney is one of the best poets I can think of writing now in the language and to see him and others concerned—overly concerned—with their literary immortality, is dismaying, or as James Joyce would have phrased it, "a cod's game."

Well, I make only this little gripe here about the end of a poem that is amazing and rather wonderful in other episodes. I think the poem ends before it ends, quite simply.

Still, the dreams that poets have of the great dead poets are powerful and sometimes unforgettable. I will just conclude with one of mine, since it is something you should never do, write your own dreams into a critical lecture. No Ph.D.-granting institution would approve of what I am about to do and that is why I feel so delighted to do it.

Once when I was living in a small studio apartment in Salt Lake, one with a Murphy bed and no color anywhere in it that wasn't gray or brown, except for some brilliantly striped, rainbow sheets that my friend Mark Strand had insisted would be just the thing for the place (though they weren't and though I had spent my last penny on them), I had a dream in which Yeats appeared. (The sheets, even with their wild colors, did not prevent me from falling asleep. It was, after all, Salt Lake City.) Anyway, I had been teaching there, a seminar on Yeats, and had the new Finneran edition of his poems with its vast acres of notes at the end of it open on the coffee table when I dozed off. When Yeats appeared, he simply walked into the place without knocking and, by way of explanation, said he didn't mean to disturb me, but that he'd left some papers there in my apartment. He had originally left them in his place in London, he said, but because of the phases of the moon and the shifting of the heavens—earth too, he shrugged—they were now here in a drawer in my tiny kitchen. He was dressed in that great white suit he had once worn and he explained that he needed these papers, needed to finish what he had been working on in them, so that he could move on to the next "bardo." No kidding, that's what he called it: "bardo." He went quietly into the kitchen and emerged again with the work in his hand and, passing by me, glanced at the new edition of his poems, the most complete and scholarly one available, open to a place where I had made a note in the margin, and paused slightly. Then he asked, "What are you reading that for?" And, looking straight at me, he said, "Passion is the only thing that matters in poetry. As a matter of fact, it is the only thing that matters in life."

Coda: A Word to the Wicked

I think that most poets labor
joyously a long time to learn the
language, to hear it, to speak it, to
write it. It is also important to read
poetry for me, to see how other
men and women have used
language during their time on earth.
Beyond that process, which goes
on all the time, there is simply a
long walk in the dark—and the
sweet electrical moment in which a
fresh poem occurs. Though this
may be the same poem that has
occurred through the ages. It may
even be the same moment, friends.

This note on poetics was originally published in the photo-essay "100 American Seducers on Their Craft and Sullen Art," *Rolling Stone,* 16 August 1973, 44.

For Further Reading

"After the Obsession with Some Beloved Figure: An Interview with Larry Levis." Interview by Leslie Kelen. *Antioch Review* 48 (1990).

"The Anatomy of Saturday Night." Preface to *The Tempo Changed, the Lights Go Up, the Partners Change,* by Thomas McAfee. St. Louis: Singing Wind, 1978.

"Four Young Poets." *New Letters* (fall 1977).

Introduction to *Each Thing We Know Is Changed Because We Know It,* by Kevin Hearle. Boise: Ahsahta Press, Boise State University, 1994.

"Not Life So Proud to Be Life: Snodgrass, Rothenberg, Bell, and the Counter-Revolution." *American Poetry Review* 18 (1989).

"Thomas Lux and *Sunday.*" *Ploughshares* (fall 1979).

"Waiting for the End of the World: W. D. Snodgrass and *The Führer Bunker.*" In *The Poetry of W. D. Snodgrass: Everything Human,* ed. Stephen Haven. Ann Arbor: University of Michigan Press, 1993.

"War as Parable and War as Fact: Zbigniew Herbert and Carolyn Forché." *American Poetry Review* (January–February 1983).

UNDER DISCUSSION
David Lehman, General Editor
Donald Hall, Founding Editor

Volumes in the Under Discussion series collect reviews and essays about individual poets. The series is concerned with contemporary American and English poets about whom the consensus has not yet been formed and the final vote has not been taken. Titles in the series include: